Ostriches,
Dung Beetles,
and Other
Spiritual
Masters

ADVANCE PRAISE

In the Genesis story of creation, we encounter God resting and viewing the whole of a magnificent creation—earth and sky, constellations and towering mountains, rocks and rivers, trees and flowers, dung beetles and human beings. The Creator smiles at the goodness of every creature. Sister Janice McLaughlin smiles, too, at all our Creator has bestowed and gently and prayerfully leads us to reflect on the "wisdom of the wild," so abundant on the African continent. The scrappy, humorous little warthog, in its resourcefulness, offers us the opportunity to pray over how we might make better use of what we have and protect earth's fragile yet beautiful environment. Rather than the power we most often associate with the lion, Sister Janice observes in this great beast joy in playfulness and spiritual renewal through relaxation "in the shade of a thorn tree." Relish this warm and wonderful book, truly a gift from Sister Janice.

—Archbishop Emeritus Desmond Mpilo Tutu

Ostriches, Dung Beetles, and Other Spiritual Masters

A Book of Wisdom from the Wild

Janice McLaughlin

ORBIS BOOKS
Maryknoll, New York

Fourth Printing, January 2011

Founded in 1970, Orbis Books endeavors to publish works that enlighten the mind, nourish the spirit, and challenge the conscience. The publishing arm of the Maryknoll Fathers and Brothers, Orbis seeks to explore the global dimensions of the Christian faith and mission, to invite dialogue with diverse cultures and religious traditions, and to serve the cause of reconciliation and peace. The books published reflect the views of their authors and do not represent the official position of the Maryknoll Society. To learn more about Maryknoll and Orbis Books, please visit our website at www.maryknollsociety.org.

Published by Orbis Books, Maryknoll, New York 10545-0308.
Manufactured in the United States of America.

An earlier edition with the same title was published in 2008 by Silveira House in Harare, Zimbabwe.

Library of Congress Cataloging-in-Publication Data

McLaughlin, Janice.
 Ostriches, dung beetles, and other spiritual masters : a book of wisdom from the wild / Janice McLaughlin.
    p. cm.
 Includes bibliographical references.
 ISBN 978-1-57075-842-3 (pbk.)
 1. Meditations. 2. Christian life—Catholic authors. 3. Christian sociology—Catholic Church—Meditations.
 4. Animals—Africa, Sub-Saharan—Miscellanea. I. Title.
 BX2182.3.M4 2009
 242—dc22
                    2009010610

What to Do

Take out all your belongings—
Furniture, clothes, crockery—
All you have since held dear
Take them all out
And return them to the forest.

Now, bring in the sky
The mountains, distant views
Of anything, the rivers, trees,
Boulders; the animals, birds
And insects—
Set them loose in your room.

Now—
Kneel down anywhere
And give thanks.

Charles Mungoshi
The Milkman Doesn't Only Deliver Milk
Baobab Books, Harare, 1998.
Used with permission of the author.

CONTENTS

Foreword by Anne Hope ix
Acknowledgments xi
Introduction 1

Baobab Tree—*Healing and Reconciliation* 3
Buffalo—*Responsible Leadership* 9
Cheetah—*Solitude* 14
Crocodile—*Patience* 19
Dung Beetle—*Perseverance* 25
Eland—*Endurance* 31
Elephant—*Communication and Community* 36
Giraffe—*Adaptation and Flexibility* 42
Greater Kudu—*Freedom* 49
Hammerkop—*Ambition* 55
Hippopotamus—*Humility and Self-Acceptance* 61
Hornbill—*Unconditional Love* 66
Impala—*Openness to Change* 71
Lion—*Playfulness and Leisure* 76
Ostrich—*Caution* 82

Owl—*Courage*   88

Porcupine (Crested)—*Justice*   94

Rhinoceros—*Stability*   100

Savanna Baboon—*Generosity*   105

Spotted Hyena—*Laughter*   111

Thorn Tree (Acacia)—*Serenity*   116

Vervet Monkey—*Friendship*   122

Warthog—*Resourcefulness*   127

Weaver Bird—*Creative Conflict Management*   132

Wildebeest—*Cooperation*   137

Zebra—*Originality*   142

Sources   148

FOREWORD

Sister Janice McLaughlin has lived a full and fascinating life. As a Maryknoll Sister she has had the opportunity to enter deeply, in a totally nonjudgmental way, into the experience and culture of a wide range of people on the African continent. Observing all with humorous eyes of faith and generous compassion, she has established warm friendships with an extraordinary range of people of different tribes and generations, from cabinet ministers to township children, freedom fighters to grandmothers who have never left their home villages. In her years in Africa she has not only become deeply attuned to all that we can learn of our Creator from nature, but has also accumulated a fund of rare wisdom applicable in daily life. She shares this with us in a highly original yet challenging way in this delightful book.

She starts each chapter with the description of an animal, a bird, or a plant—but not the ones one might expect. Many of us have probably been profoundly moved by the loyalty of a dog, been awestruck by its capacity to enter empathetically into our feelings, to share our joys and sorrows, and to comfort us simply with their presence. (A well-known theologian, Matthew Fox, has said that his dog is his "spiritual director.") But have you ever thought what you might learn from an ostrich, a warthog, or a dung beetle? Janice tells us things we probably never knew about these and other creatures. Then she goes on to tell stories of some of her own experiences, such as three weeks in prison in Ian Smith's Rhodesia, which she describes as "the best retreat I ever made." From giraffes she learned flexibility and adaptation to new and different values, much needed as she spent time in a Maasai *boma*, or homestead. From a pride of lions she learned the importance of relaxation and playfulness. From the hippo, self-acceptance.

With a few simple quotations Janice links the "wisdom from the wild" to the words and the life of Jesus. Her reflections on passages from the Gospels make us realize that her extraordinary capacity for friendship and her ability to relate empathetically to people of such different cultures are born of deep spiritual insight, and of her close relationship to God. Though the context of her life may seem exotic to those who have lived comfortably in suburbia, the lessons she has learned are relevant for all of us.

Anne Hope
Cape Town, June 2008
(Co-author with Sally Timmel of *Training for Transformation*,
co-founder of the Grail Centre, Kleinmond, South Africa,
and recipient of the Steve Biko Award, 2001)

ACKNOWLEDGMENTS

Without many helping hands, hearts, and heads this book would never have been completed. Park rangers and game guides in Zimbabwe and Botswana increased my knowledge and fed my interest in the behaviors and habits of wildlife: Albert Paradzai (Gonarozhou), Jacob Bangidzai (Victoria Falls), Edwin Tuelo and Nicodemus Modimoosi (Chope, Botswana), and Rudolph (Mbizi).

Zimbabwean artist Charles Chazike drew the illustrations of the elephant, giraffe, hornbill, and weaver bird before his untimely death in December 2006. Justin Gope from Mozambique, another talented artist and friend, stepped in to complete the illustrations.

Sisters Teresa Baldini and Grace Myerjack from the Maryknoll contemplative community read the first draft and told me that what I have learned in Africa would be of interest to others. Anne Hope, my longtime friend and mentor, readily agreed to write the foreword while my housemates, Sr. Jeongmi Lee, our dog, and our cat, gave me daily doses of love and laughter and the courage to share these personal reflections with others.

As a longtime reader and promoter of Orbis books, I am proud to join their list of distinguished authors. I am grateful to Robert Ellsberg, who accepted my manuscript for publication, and Sue Perry, who performed her editorial magic to make this edition so attractive and readable.

Thanks to all of you for your encouragement, advice, and support.

INTRODUCTION

For more than thirty years, I have reveled in the breathtaking beauty of the African continent. From Kilimanjaro to Cape Town, I have been privileged to interact with its people, who live in harmony with nature, and with the abundance of wildlife that make Africa such a Garden of Eden. This is also where I have experienced the deepest connection and communion with the Creator of such bounty.

I have learned to appreciate the close links between nature and culture on this continent. In the Shona and Ndebele cultures of Zimbabwe, for instance, each person is given a totem at birth. A totem is a guardian animal spirit that is supposed to protect and guide its bearer. It is a means of identification among peoples and is often used when one person is introduced to another. Those with the same totem immediately feel at home with one another and start to share as if they are blood relations. One is forbidden to eat the meat of one's totem and is prohibited from marrying someone with the same totem. Sometimes individuals emulate the characteristics of their totem spirit. A child who has the rabbit as its totem, for instance, might be very clever and mischievous while one with the buffalo totem might be strong and dependable.

The Kenyans with whom I worked for seven years gave me the butterfly totem because I was always on the move, flitting from one project and one place to another. That is still an accurate description! I have also come to treasure the butterfly as a symbol of the resurrection as I have looked into the eyes of death so often and seen the yearning for release from pain and suffering and hope for a new and better life. I too have been reborn countless times through the daily small deaths that are part of every life—letting go of personal ambition, plans, and dreams of glory to embrace the miracles that caring for others and compassion make possible.

I never tire of visiting the many and varied national parks on this continent and am fascinated by the accounts of park rangers, describing the habits of the wildlife and their environment. As I learned more about animal behavior, I began to see parallels with the behavior of human beings. I started to wonder if nature has special lessons for us; lessons that we so often fail to heed in our busyness to accomplish something, to go somewhere, or to seem important.

As I wondered if others might also find something worthwhile in the wisdom of the wild, I began to collect information about the wildlife I had seen and to draw parallels with my own or other people's experience. This book is the result. Each chapter begins with a description of a specific animal's behavior or the traits of birds, insects, and even trees. It goes on to recount an experience I've had that draws on this natural wisdom. Each chapter ends with some quotations from Scripture, and a few questions for reflection or discussion, and suggestions for action.

I share this wisdom with gratitude for my parents and all the guides in my life who have helped me to hear, see, and appreciate the message that is waiting in all of creation.

Throughout I have used the eighteenth edition of the Christian Community Bible published by Claretian Publications (1995). Although I have tried to use inclusive language throughout, in some cases I have failed.

BAOBAB TREE

Healing and Reconciliation

Looking like it was planted upside down, the baobab thrives in hot, dry climates where nothing else will grow. Its fruit is the tartar that is used in various toothpastes and creams, while the pods can be used as sponges and its bark can be beaten into mats or clothing. This versatile tree has another distinct advantage. When a disease strikes it, the plant explodes from within to rid itself of the sickness. This leaves it with huge gaping holes in its trunk that looks as if an elephant has attacked and scooped out the inside. Though it looks ugly, the baobab is healthy once more.

In 1991 Michael Lapsley, an Anglican priest from Australia who has spent most of his adult life in southern Africa, received a parcel bomb in the mail at his home in Harare, Zimbabwe. As he leaned over to open it, the parcel exploded, leaving him wounded and bleeding on the floor. When I went to see him in the hospital in Harare a few days after the bombing, he had two bandaged stumps where his hands had been and an open hole that had once held his eye. But he was smiling as he told me, "The Boers made a mistake. They took away my hands and my eye but I still have my mouth. That is my strongest weapon and I will continue to use it to condemn racism."

Lapsley testified before South Africa's Truth and Reconciliation Commission, which

was set up in 1995 to heal the wounds of decades of apartheid and guerrilla warfare. In his testimony, he pleaded for the person who sent him the parcel bomb to come forward so he could forgive him. Instead of clinging to hatred and a desire for revenge, Lapsley, like the baobab, was expelling the bitterness so he would be healed. Perhaps in the process, his attacker would also be healed.

In his book on reconciliation, Robert Schreiter claims that in most cases it is the victims of violence and trauma who take the initiative to reach out and forgive their attackers. When I first read this, I protested vehemently, claiming that this would be like blaming the victim for their wounds and wounding them a second time. Only gradually, as I learned to let go of small hurts that had been done to me, did I begin to see the wisdom of this theory. If I hold on to the pain and cling to my woundedness, I hand over my power and identity to my attacker. I live in his or her shadow every day, plotting and planning how I will get even. My life then revolves around seeking revenge, making the other person pay, showing that I am tougher and stronger and can outdo him or her in inflicting pain. Whether I fantasize about inflicting psychological or physical pain, my life becomes a living nightmare and I become enmeshed in a web of self-destruction and despair.

Nelson Mandela, the first president of a democratic multiracial South Africa, spent more than twenty years in prison but emerged without rancor or bitterness. He became a model of reconciliation in a country that had experienced forty-four years of a brutal apartheid system that deprived black people of their rights in their own country. Yet Mandela did not preach hatred and revenge. In his autobiography, *Long Walk to Freedom*, he recounts how he was able to survive in prison by finding the spark of humanity in his guards. "I always knew that deep down in every human heart, there was mercy and generosity," he wrote. "No one is born hating another person because of the color of his skin, or his background, or his religion. People must learn to hate, and if they can learn to hate, they can be taught to love, for love comes more naturally to the human heart than its opposite. Even in the grimmest times in prison, when my comrades and I were pushed to our limits, I would see a glimmer of humanity in one of our guards, perhaps just for a second, but it was enough to reassure me and keep me going. Man's goodness is a flame that can be hidden but never extinguished."*

This ability to overcome the urge for revenge enabled Mandela to build a new nation from the ruins of apartheid. He was able to unify all races and tribes in this formerly divided country. In his book *God Has a Dream: A Vision of Hope for Our Time*, Bishop Desmond Tutu rightly describes it as a miracle. "Who in their right mind could ever have imagined South Africa to be an example of anything but the most ghastly awfulness, of how not to govern a nation? We were destined for perdition and were plucked out of total annihilation. We were a hopeless case if ever there was one. We succeeded not because we were smart. Patently not so. Not because we were particularly virtuous. We succeeded because God wanted us to succeed. . . . This is the principle of transfiguration at work. And so no situation is utterly hopeless, utterly untransfigurable."[†]

The miracle of South Africa's transfiguration is a powerful reminder that healing and

---

* Nelson Mandela, *Long Walk to Freedom: The Autobiography of Nelson Mandela* (Boston: Little, Brown, 1994), 542.

[†] Desmond Tutu, *God Has a Dream: A Vision of Hope for Our Time* (Doubleday/Image, 2005), 125.

reconciliation can take place in even the most hopeless situations. Like the baobab tree, let us learn to expel the anger and bitterness we carry through life and embrace the possibility of change.

Scripture

"You have heard it was said: love your neighbor and hate your enemy. But this I tell you: Love your enemies and pray for those who persecute you, so that you may be children of your Father in Heaven." (Matthew 5:43-45)

"Then Peter asked him, 'Lord, how many times must I forgive the offences of my brother or sister? Seven times?' Jesus answered, 'No, not seven times, but seventy-seven times.'" (Matthew 18:21)

"If you go to give your gift at the altar and remember that your brother or sister has a grudge against you, go first to be reconciled and then come to offer your gift." (Matthew 5:23)

Reflection

1. How do you feel when you have been wronged?
2. Have you ever sought revenge against someone who wronged you? Did it make you feel better?

3. Do you know people like Mandela or Michael Lapsley who have forgiven their enemies? What have you learned from them?
4. Have you ever given up the need to seek revenge when you have been wronged? Why did you do it? How did you do it?

Action

1. This week reach out to someone who you feel has hurt you and try to discuss it with them, seeking understanding and reconciliation.
2. Reach out to someone you may have hurt through word or deed. Let them know how you are feeling and ask what you can do to restore the relationship.

BUFFALO

Responsible Leadership

One of the "big five," the African buffalo ranks with the elephant, the lion, the rhino, and the leopard as the most sought-after animals on the African continent because they are dangerous, powerful, and fearless. The buffalo, in fact, ranks second to the hippo as the most dangerous because it often gores or tramples to death unsuspecting humans who cross its path by mistake. Large herds of buffalo are a common sight on the African plain. The African buffalo is related to the Asian and American bison, as well as to the common cow, but its ancestry is unknown. While cattle have not adapted well to the harsh African climate and require human intervention to survive, the buffalo is at home in a variety of climates and terrains although it needs large amounts of water and vegetation to survive. Large herds of buffalo can be found throughout eastern, central, and southern Africa in woodlands, flood plains, savannas, and swamps. Its strong teeth and flexible tongue allow the buffalo to scoop up the long, tough grass that others can't chew or digest.

Sociable animals, African buffalo are nonterritorial and live in mixed herds of male and female that number from fifty to one thousand beasts. When they are too old to breed, the males move out and join bachelor herds to give the young males a better chance to mate. The herds are subdivided into clans of a dozen or more related cows and their offspring.

Each clan has its own leader or pathfinder that guides the group to water and pasture. The pathfinder walks in front, while others file behind, often in a single line. The leader knows how to avoid danger and how to find water and grass even in times of drought. Without a leader, buffalo would perish in a fruitless search for food and drink in the arid plains where they roam.

Sometimes I facilitate leadership workshops in Zimbabwe and Kenya where we ask participants to name someone who was an outstanding leader or role model in their life. We ask them to recall those who played a positive role as well as those who had a negative influence on them. Many name parents or relatives who raised them. Some point to teachers or religious persons who encouraged or influenced them in their growth and development. Others single out well-known figures or national heroes such as Nelson Mandela or Bishop Desmond Tutu of South Africa.

As we explore the qualities of these personal guides, we usually find that they share certain common traits or characteristics: they put the good of others before their own interests; they are good listeners; they are courageous; and they have a positive outlook on life.

In contrast, those who played a negative role for participants are described as selfish, cruel, and uncaring. Jesus was very clear about his vision of leadership. He knelt down and washed the feet of his followers, telling them that they must do likewise. In another example, Jesus contrasts the behavior of earthly leaders with his own and sets out an ideal for his followers: "The kings of the pagan nations rule over them as lords, and the most hardhearted rulers claim the title, 'Gracious Lord.' But not so with you; let the greatest among you become as the youngest, and the leader as the servant. . . . I am among you as the one who serves" (Luke 22:25-27).

Julius Nyerere, the first president of independent Tanzania, was such a leader. Affectionately called "Mwalimu," or Teacher, Nyerere did not crave wealth and power but was humble, good-humored, and willing to admit his mistakes. I first met him in 1970 when he came to Maryknoll in New York to address a general assembly of our community, which is held every six years. He called on us to live and work with the people, not as bosses but as companions. "Only by sharing work, hardships, knowledge, persecution, and progress can the Church contribute to our growth," he said. "And this means sharing in every sense as 'members one of another.' For if the Church is not part of our poverty, and part of our struggle against poverty and injustice, then it is not part of us." He encouraged us to leave our institutional ministries and go live and work with the people in the *ujamaa* villages. "The poor and oppressed should come to you not for alms," he stressed, "but for support against injustice" (*Freedom and Development*, pp. 213-28).

When he stepped down as president, Nyerere returned to his rural home to farm. He jokingly called himself an itinerant peasant—when he wasn't in the village he was traveling to international meetings and conferences to share his vast experience and wisdom. He did not cling to the trappings of power but lived simply. On one visit to the United Nations, some Tanzania residents in New York brought him a coat for the cool weather since he came dressed only in sandals and his trademark safari suit. He reluctantly tried on the coat and then handed it to a Maryknoll sister who also had come to see him. "It fits Sr. Jean better than me," he announced with a twinkle in his eye. "She should have it!"

Thanks to his wise leadership, Tanzania is a unified and peaceful country that serves as a model and inspiration to other African nations. If the Catholic community in Tanzania has its way, Julius Nyerere will be the first political leader to be declared a saint. Each generation and every nation and people needs a pathfinder like Mwalimu who can point the way to a better future for all. Each of us is called to be a person of integrity, who lives up to our ideals and provides responsible and credible leadership to those who come after us.

Scripture

> "When Jesus was finished washing their feet, he put on his garment again, went back to the table and said to them, 'Do you understand what I have done to you? You call me Master and Lord, and you are right, for so I am. If I, then, Your Lord and Master, have washed your feet, you also must wash one another's feet. I have just given you an example that as I have done, you also may do.'" (John 13:12-15)

"One blind person cannot lead another one; if one does, both will fall into a ditch. No pupil is greater than one's teacher; but every pupil, when completing the training, will be like the teacher." (Luke 6:39-40)

Reflection

1. Do you know a "servant leader" who has inspired you? Who was it? How did they inspire you?
2. Have you been in a leadership role? If so, how did you treat others? How did you expect them to treat you?

Action

1. Read the biography or autobiography of a leader who has inspired you. Then discuss it with others and see what you can learn from this example.
2. Introduce a course in ethical leadership at your local church, business, or school. Include case studies of outstanding leaders.

CHEETAH

Solitude

Built for speed, with light bones and long limbs, the cheetah is the world's fastest land animal. Running at a top speed of seventy miles per hour, cheetahs rarely miss their prey. Unlike most wild cats, except their leopard cousin, they hunt and live alone unless they are mating and raising their cubs.

It is rare for wild animals to be alone since there is safety in numbers. With its sharp eyesight and incredible speed, however, the cheetah seems able to fend for itself. The young leave home at one and a half years after learning how to hunt. Brothers sometimes live together to enlarge the territory they control, enhancing their mating prospects, but young females follow their mother's example and live on their own.

Solitude is no longer appreciated in the fast-paced and noisy world of North America. Lone commuters in planes, trains, and subways chat on their cell phones, send text messages, or listen to music on their iPods. Even walking on the street, many people are intently talking to their phones or have earpieces connecting them to something else. At home, singles tend to turn on the radio and television to keep them company in the evening, and families often do the same. Children spend hours on the Internet or the telephone or playing hand-held video games.

How often do we take a day off from the noise and busyness just to be quiet and appreciate the world around us? Are we actually able to sit quietly for thirty minutes a day, turning off the constant bombardment of thoughts and images? Can we be alone with ourselves without the distraction of radio, television, or Internet? Do we ever take time by ourselves to reflect on our daily experience?

I suspect we might feel that we were wasting time if we did any of the above. Yet it is in solitude and silence that God most often speaks to us. I sometimes envy the herders of sheep and cattle in Africa who spend each day alone with the animals in the fields. As I watch them reclining on the grass while the sheep and cattle feed, I often wonder whether they enjoy their solitary pursuit or if they're wishing to live in a fast-paced world like ours.

Jesus lived in a preindustrial world like these African herders and used stories of fishers and farmers to convey his message of the kingdom of God. He often took time out from his active ministry to go off alone to pray, and he taught his disciples to do the same.

When I joined the Maryknoll Sisters in 1961, we had many monastic customs, including a culture of silence. We seldom talked at meals or at work. Only one hour each day was set aside for conversing with others. Listening to the radio and television was not permitted. While this was an extreme example that I would not recommend, it taught me the discipline of being alone, of being comfortable with my own company. To this day, while I value community life, I need time to be by myself. This is the time that enables me to stay tuned to God and to get replenished for the following day.

Bishop Desmond Tutu of South Africa is a very engaged and outgoing person. His schedule is full of meetings, important appointments, and speaking engagements around the world. When asked how he manages to do all this, he said that he takes time for prayer and solitude each day and sets aside a week each month for a silent retreat. With his inimitable humor, he explained that he felt a real physical discomfort if he failed to spend time in quiet meditation each day—"It is worse than having forgotten to brush my teeth."*

If such a busy person can take the time to be alone with God, why can't we?

Scripture

"Very early in the morning, before daylight, Jesus went off to a lonely place where he prayed. Simon and the others went out, too, searching for him; and when they found him they said, 'Everybody is looking for you.'" (Mark 1:35-37)

---

* For more on Bishop Tutu's spirituality, see Desmond Tutu, *God Has a Dream: A Vision of Hope for Our Time* (New York: Doubleday/Image, 2005). This quotation is from p. 100.

"The apostles returned and reported to Jesus all they had done and taught. Then he said to them, 'Go off by yourselves to a remote place and have some rest.' For there were so many people coming and going that the apostles had no time even to eat. And they went away in a boat to a secluded area by themselves." (Mark 6:30-32)

"On reaching the place, he [Elijah] came to the cave and stayed in it. . . . Then Yahweh said, 'Go up and stand on the mount, waiting for Yahweh.' And Yahweh passed by. There was first a windstorm, wild wind which rent the mountains and broke the rocks into pieces before Yahweh, but Yahweh was not in the wind. After the storm, an earthquake, but Yahweh was not in the earthquake. After the earthquake, a fire, but Yahweh was not in the fire. After the fire, the murmur of a gentle breeze. When Elijah perceived it, he covered his face with his cloak, went out and stood at the entrance of the cave." (1 Kings 19:9-13)

Reflection

1. How do you feel when you are alone? What do you do?
2. How do you replenish yourself after a busy day? A busy week?

Action

1. Make a formal retreat for a weekend or a full week.
2. Learn about centering prayer (see the writings of Anthony de Mello, John Main, Thomas Keating, or Basil Pennington) and try to practice it for at least fifteen minutes a day.

3. Before going to bed, quietly reflect on the day, giving thanks for the blessings you received. In the morning before going to work, reflect on the day ahead, asking for wisdom and guidance.

4. Take a walk by yourself in a park, in the woods, or by a river or lake. Go slowly and contemplate your surroundings.

CROCODILE

Patience

The African crocodile is both respected and feared. It is one of the most dangerous reptiles on earth but is also very useful. Its skin can be made into beautiful products such as belts, shoes, and bags, and its meat is more tender and tasty than chicken. Crocodiles have enormous patience and when hungry can wait half submerged in water for days at a time, until an unsuspecting animal or human being approaches. Then a crocodile opens its huge jaws and attacks with such speed and agility that the victim rarely escapes. Their patience seems to have rewarded them with longevity. Crocodiles can live as long as 110 years and grow up to eighteen feet in length, a clear testimony to their survival skills. Scientists have established that their ancestors lived with the dinosaurs from 135 to 65 million years ago.

A floating crocodile can be mistaken for a log, so silent and still are they. I can barely stay still for three or four minutes. In spite of spending more than thirty years on the African continent, I find myself fretting and fuming when I have to wait. And yet the African continent is a great test and teacher of patience. One waits in queues at the bank, the post office, the grocery store. One waits months for a work permit. One waits hours, sometimes days, for people to arrive for appointments. In a land with few clocks and watches, time is not measured in seconds, minutes, and hours. Time seems to be lived rather than measured.

When I first arrived in Kenya in 1970, I was always rushing to accomplish things in my post as communications secretary for the Catholic Bishops' Conference. One day when I felt under a lot of pressure I urged my secretary, Helen Maeke, to complete some letters before the end of the working day. "What time is it?" I asked anxiously, wanting to make a 4:30 deadline. Helen made a great show of looking down at her bare wrist as if she were consulting a watch. "Plenty of time, no hurry," she replied with a straight face.

I realized that I had already forgotten the lessons I had learned at language school only a few months before. The first Swahili proverb that we young missioners, fresh out of our novitiate, were taught was *Haraka,*

haraka, haina baraka. Rush, rush, there is no blessing. The second proverb we learned was similar: *Pole, pole, ndio mwendo*. Slowly, slowly is the way forward.

I have never forgotten these words—but I rarely practice them. So ingrained are my lifelong habits of getting things done, not wasting time, and accomplishing goals that I find it difficult to sit still like the crocodile and wait for whatever God sends my way. I realize that it is largely a matter of control. I want to make things happen my way, and not let them happen by surprise.

When I first went to Mozambique in 1978 to work with refugees from Zimbabwe, I was forced to spend most of my time waiting. I was not yet known or accepted by the different departments of the Zimbabwe African National Union (ZANU) that were running the camps. Each morning I would get up early, walk to the ZANU offices and try to see the various leaders of each department—health, welfare, education, and so on. Each evening I would walk back to the apartment where I was staying, totally frustrated and annoyed because I had waited in vain. There were days when I wanted to get on the next plane and leave Mozambique. "They don't need me or want me. What am I doing here?" I frequently asked myself.

One day I changed my attitude and decided that the waiting itself was valuable. I went to the offices in a cheerful mood and started chatting with the secretaries and the young security guards. As I made friends with them, they started confiding in me and inviting me to share meals with them. Then I was invited to work in the education office, preparing books and training manuals for printing. I was not in charge and was rarely consulted but I shared the daily tasks in the office and came to know and respect the young freedom fighters who had left their homes and families in order to liberate their country.

Their days were as monotonous as mine. Their work was routine. They had poor food and accommodations, but they worked with commitment and courage. When I asked one of the women leaders in the education department the meaning of it all, she replied simply, "We do it for love."

The Buddhist monk and activist Thich Nhat Hanh has popularized the Buddhist practice of mindfulness in his public lectures and retreats throughout the world. I recall that when I first read his book on the subject, I was very impatient and dismissive. "How can focusing on my breathing make a difference?" I complained. I prided myself that I could do two or three things at the same time, never wasting a minute. When my father was dying, I sat at his bedside in the hospital and listened to Shona language tapes until one day my father sat up and asked me, "Why did you come? You could be learning Shona in Zimbabwe." I put my book away and became present to my father. For the next few days, his breathing was my breathing, and his pain became my pain. When he passed peacefully away, I was holding his hand and praying with him, a blessing I will always treasure. But one doesn't need to lose a loved one to learn the importance of living in the present moment.

After independence, when we all returned to Zimbabwe from Mozambique, my friend and companion in ZANU's Education Department, Irene (Ropa) Mahamba, wrote me a farewell poem that reads in part:

> Maybe as we part temporarily
> You could remember sometimes
> That as rain falls
> And water seeps in through the soil

> Only in the green grass and flowers
> Does the soil show its appreciation and thanks. . . .

I treasure this poem and its meaning. I will never be as patient as the crocodile or as my Zimbabwean friends. But I no longer judge those who appear to do nothing but sit in the sun all day. Nor do I judge a culture as lazy and backward because it moves at a slower pace than mine. I at least have learned to stop imposing my cultural values on others, even though I still practice them myself. I yearn for the day when I will be like the gentle rain soaking the earth and bringing forth new life without a lot of effort and stress.

Scripture

"Look at the wild flowers: they do not spin or weave; but I tell you, even Solomon with all his wealth was not clothed as one of these. If God so clothes the grass in the fields, which is alive today and tomorrow is thrown into the oven, how much more will he clothe you, people of little faith. . . . Stop worrying." (Luke 12:27-29; Matthew 6:26-30)

"Look at the birds of the air; they do not sow, they do not harvest and do not store food in barns, and yet your heavenly father feeds them. Are you not worth much more than birds?" (Matthew 6:26)

"A farmer scatters seed upon the soil. Whether the sower is asleep or awake, be it day or night, the seed sprouts and grows, s/he knows not how. The soil produces of itself; first the blade, then the ear, then the full grain in the ear. And when it is ripe for harvesting they take the sickle for the cutting: the time for harvest has come." (Mark 4:26-29)

Reflection

1. What makes you impatient? How does it feel? What do you do?
2. Have you met people who exude a sense of calm and peace? How do they do this?
3. Have you tried to practice "mindfulness"? How does it feel for you?

Action

1. Sit still for ten minutes and focus on your breathing. Put all thoughts out of your mind.
2. The next time that you have to wait, use the time to meditate on the gift of life.

DUNG BEETLE

Perseverance

There is hardly a more comical sight than the humble dung beetle pushing a ball of dung more than twice its size. The beetle perches on top, balancing like an acrobat, while moving the precious ball that is both food and nest for her eggs. Using the shovel-like front part of her head, the female beetle carves out a chunk of dung about the size of a ping-pong ball. Then she uses her stout front legs to shape it into a perfect sphere, making it easier to push to an underground tunnel where she may deposit several balls, laying a single egg in each. The hatched larvae will feed on it. These larvae, in turn, serve as food for a number of birds and small animals. There are more than eighteen hundred species of dung beetles in Africa alone. They help to spread the seeds that were ingested by various animals and are expelled in their droppings and are ready to sprout when the rains come. What an ingenious way to replenish the plant life of the African plain!

I have watched beetles pushing a ball up a hill, only to have it slip and roll to the bottom. Like the Greek myth of Sisyphus, the beetle returns to the bottom and starts all over again, and again, and again—never giving up until she reaches the top with the dung ball intact. Such perseverance is a reminder that achievement takes effort and persistence. If we give up when we encounter obstacles, we will never reach our goal.

The Shona word for perseverance, *kushinga*, comes from the same root as *kushingisa*, which means to strengthen. Isn't it true that when we persevere, we become stronger and more confident?

Zimbabweans are experts at persevering. During the liberation war (1968-1980), Zimbabweans learned to live with sanctions, and as a result most goods, including fuel, were rationed. Because the country had to learn how to produce its own goods when it could no longer import them from outside, the Zimbabwean economy actually grew stronger. Zimbabweans also learned devious strategies such as outwitting the sanctions by importing and exporting through friendly third parties who were willing, at a price, to assist their neighbors.

In recent years, Zimbabwe is once more under siege, this time from its own government.

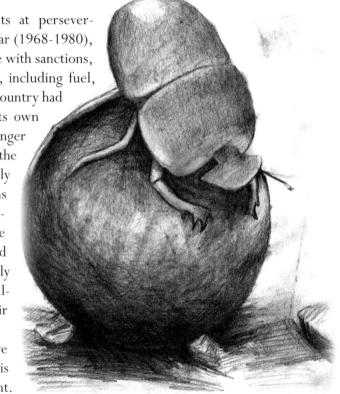

With food, fuel, and electricity in short supply, outsiders wonder why Zimbabweans don't take to the streets to protest. In addition to fear of the consequences, I believe that Zimbabweans have simply learned how to survive in tough times. Their ability to persevere amid immense hardships impresses even the most hardened cynic. While one might wish that the people would take more risks and be more outspoken about their plight, I admire their stoic acceptance of what is and their belief that things will one day change for the better.

Their great faith in a God who cares also helps them through the hard times. "*Mwari anoziva*" (God knows), they say of all problems and injustices, and many children are named *Isheanesu* (God is with us). Such faith, like the faith of the prophets of the Old Testament or the faith of Job, who, though sorely tempted, never blamed God for his problems or stopped believing and trusting in God, is a great challenge to Christians everywhere.

It was recently revealed that Mother Teresa of Calcutta went for many years with few signs of God's love and care for her. Yet, through this "dark night of the soul," as St. John of the Cross called such periods of spiritual drought, she continued to spend her life in service to the most downtrodden of Indian society. She persevered in her vocation in spite of the lack of any spiritual consolation or reward. Jesus also felt abandoned by his Father at the most critical time in his life, as he faced his imminent brutal death in the garden of Gethsemane. "Take this cup from me," he prayed. "Not my will but thine be done," he concluded, as he accepted the suffering that lay ahead.

This kind of perseverance and acceptance of earthly failure and pain is the hallmark of exceptional human beings and saints! Nelson Mandela persevered for twenty-seven long years in prison without giving up his dream for a non-racial society and for liberation for the people of South Africa. When I visited Robben Island where Mandela was imprisoned, the former political prisoner who was our guide told of his own painful journey. He spent twelve years in prison and his father was shot and crippled for life because of the political activities of his son. Yet this former freedom fighter spoke of forgiveness and reconciliation rather than revenge. Such attitudes can build a new world of unity, equality, and harmony rather than the present world of wars, poverty, and inequality.

Two Nobel Prize winners in 2007 were individuals who had persevered over the years in their chosen fields of endeavor. Doris Lessing, the Zimbabwean author who won the prize for literature, turned eighty-eight a few days after being informed of the honor she had finally been accorded. A writer most of her adult life, her African stories vividly capture the harsh injustice of life in a colonial society. Al Gore, a former U.S. vice president and presidential candidate, was awarded the Peace Prize for his work on global warming. In his award-winning film, *An Inconvenient Truth*, Gore reveals that he became interested in the environment while a university student. Since then, he has devoted thirty years of his life to creating awareness about the perils of global warming. Both these Nobel winners illustrate the importance of not giving up.

They remind us that change does not happen by accident. Improvements don't come overnight. If we want to make a difference in the world, we must be prepared to work hard and long. We cannot give up when we meet obstacles and hardships but, like the dung beetle, we must be prepared to try again and again until we succeed. "A path is made by walking the same way many times," says a Tonga proverb. Can we persevere and make new paths to a better world for all?

Scripture

"Stay awake, then, for you do not know on what day your Lord will come. Just think about this: if the owner of the house knew that the thief would come by night around a certain hour, the owner would stay awake to prevent anyone from breaking into the house. So be alert, for the Son of Man will come at the hour you least expect." (Matthew 24:42-44)

"Be ready, dressed for service, and keep your lamps lit, like people waiting for their master to return from the wedding. As soon as he comes and knocks, they will open to him. Happy are those servants whom the master finds wide awake when he comes." (Luke 12:35-36)

Reflection

1. Have you had an experience of persevering in an endeavor or a project that was not easy for you? What did you learn from this experience?
2. Have you experienced giving up when things got too tough? What did you learn?
3. Have you witnessed individuals or groups who have persevered and achieved their goals? What does this teach us?

Action

1. Get involved with others in a cause in which you believe.

2. Persevere in a project to bring change in your local neighborhood, church, or workplace.
3. Read one of Doris Lessing's books. Discuss it with others.
4. Watch *An Inconvenient Truth* with others; then make a commitment to do something to halt global warming.

ELAND

Endurance

Elands are the largest of the seventy-two species of antelopes on the African continent. An adult male can weigh up to two thousand pounds. Because of their size, elands are slow and cannot outrun their predators—the lion and the hyena—but they have a distinct advantage over many faster and stronger animals that enables them to endure harsh environments where others succumb to heat and drought. Elands have a unique internal cooling system that sends their temperatures soaring by as much 13.5 degrees F on the hottest days. They simply store heat, rather than dissipating it through panting and losing water in the process. The stored heat gradually fades in the cooler night air.

A second cooling mechanism involves rapid, rhythmic breathing with their mouths closed. This nasal panting cools blood flowing close to the surface in a rich capillary network, which in turn cools the blood that flows to the brain. This built-in air conditioning enables elands to live in semi-desert and mountainous areas and to endure unbearable heat and periods of drought that claim the lives of many smaller animals. Their endurance helps them to survive.

Endurance is not highly valued in affluent societies that can afford all kinds of comforts and conveniences to keep pain and discomfort at bay. Endurance appears negative—why put up with things that can be avoided? But all societies do not have the luxury of avoiding hardships, and all people worldwide, rich and poor alike, must endure the loss of loved ones as well as the sorrow of their own diminishment and death. We all face disappointment at one time or another, when things don't go as we planned or when those we love let us down.

We can endure gracefully, like the eland, or we can resist, exhausting ourselves and all those around us. A friend and his wife in Tafara, a Zimbabwean township on the eastern edge of Harare, taught me the beauty of endurance as well as its source. Tonderai was a leader of the Catholic Youth Association (CYA) at the local parish. He welcomed Sr. Kathryn Shannon and me when we came to live in the township in 1986. He organized all the youth to assist us and encouraged them to participate in income-generating projects. He was one of the first to get a job on completing high school, to be married in the church, and to raise a family, two boys and a girl. He was also the first to get sick with a strange disease that caused rapid weight loss and incessant coughing. Although HIV and AIDS were attacking many Zimbabweans, especially youth, there was not much information or knowledge about it. Little appeared in the mass media, and the newspapers simply referred to "a long illness" when a well-known person succumbed to the fatal disease.

When I visited Tonderai at his home after he became sick, I was shocked to see how weak and thin he was, but I was greeted with his familiar wide smile and genuine welcome. Each visit I watched helplessly as he grew weaker and weaker. His wife cared for him lovingly and tirelessly. Neither of them complained or lamented their fate.

On one of my last visits, Tonderai told me that a group of men and women from the parish came each evening to sit with him and pray. A radiant smile lit up his emaciated face as he exclaimed, "I never knew they loved me so much." He died a few days later, surrounded by friends and family who loved him and cared for him up to the last. The tributes paid him at his wake and funeral attested to the respect and love in which he was held. His wife continues to work tirelessly to send their three children to school. "I miss him every day," she recently told me. "No one can ever replace him in my life."

The example of this couple helped to remove some of the stigma surrounding the disease. No one blamed Tonderai or his wife nor speculated on how he might have contracted the illness. Rather, they rallied around to support them and to accompany them in their pain and suffering. The whole parish learned an important lesson.

Since then, I have witnessed hundreds more deaths from AIDS and other preventable diseases such as cholera, malaria, pneumonia, and tuberculosis. Not all patients have accepted their plight as stoically as Tonderai nor have they received such loving support from their family and friends. I learned that a loving community, like the cooling system of the eland, helps people to endure great pain and hardships and to reach out to others who are also suffering. A world without caring and compassion is a diminished place that leads to depression and despair.

We cannot long endure without love. "My yoke is sweet and my burden light," Jesus told his followers after warning them that his way is not an easy path. It seems a contradiction. Anyone who has cared for another, however, knows how rewarding it can be to forget self in service to others. The L'Arche communities that were founded by Jean Vanier to provide a caring environment for the mentally handicapped witness to the healing power of love—for the caregivers as well as for their patients. These communities put into practice the great paradox of Christianity: "If you choose to save your life, you will lose it; and if you lose your life for my sake and for the sake of the Gospel, you will save it" (Mark 8:35).

"So often, we run away from suffering, our own and that of others," says Vanier. "We do not realize that Jesus is hidden in those who suffer. He calls us to bear and offer both our pain and the suffering of others. . . . You will recognize Jesus, hidden in people's hearts, especially in those who are weak and broken. Thus, you will no longer be alone."* Tonderai and his wife learned this lesson. So can we.

Scripture

"We prove we are true ministers of God in every way by our endurance in so many trials, in hardships, afflictions, floggings, imprisonment, riots, fatigue, sleepless

---

* Jean Vanier, *I Walk with Jesus* (New York: Paulist Press, 1986).

nights and days of hunger. . . . We appear to be afflicted, but we remain happy; we seem to be poor, but we enrich many; apparently we have nothing, but we possess everything!" (2 Corinthians 6:4, 10)

"Many run, but only one gets the prize. Run, therefore, intending to win it, as athletes who impose upon themselves a rigorous discipline. Yet for them the wreath is of laurels which wither, while for us, it does not wither." (1 Corinthians 9:24-25)

Reflection

1. Have you ever had to endure a hardship or painful experience? What did you learn from this?
2. Have you helped others who have been going through hard times? What did you learn?

Action

1. Volunteer at a hospice program for the terminally ill or visit the sick in your parish.
2. Learn more about HIV-AIDS and support one of the many organizations that help those who are ill or the children who have been orphaned.

ELEPHANT

Communication and Community

The gentle giants of the savanna are the most sociable of animals. They live in family groups that provide companionship and meet their social needs. Safety and survival are not so much a concern when size eliminates most other species as predators. The two greatest dangers to these majestic mammals are humans, who kill for the coveted ivory tusks, and drought, which brings starvation and death to an animal that eats approximately 330 pounds of vegetation a day.

Sister elephants travel together with their children and are led by a matriarch. Female offspring remain with their mothers and aunts for the first twenty-five years of their lives, before going off to start their own clans. Males usually leave the family herd after fifteen years when they join other young bulls and begin the search for a mate. Rarely does one encounter a lone elephant save for the rogue bull who is chased away from the herd for his aggressive, anti-social behavior, and the aged patriarch who goes off alone to spend his last years in solitude, without being a burden to the community.

A group of young elephants at play is a joy to behold as they romp in the water or roll in the mud, devising numerous games to entertain themselves and their age-mates.

Not only do elephants live in community but they also communicate over long distances. An elephant in distress can call for help for a radius of over eighteen and a half miles, using infrasound signals that only they can hear. Perhaps they also communicate good news such as a birth or the location of a lush watering hole or a field of succulent grass.

It is said that we humans are also communitarian animals who find our fulfillment and identity through interaction with others. The family is our first community and the foundation for our relations with others. It is a proven fact that children who have not known love when they were young find it difficult to engage in loving relationships as they grow up.

Jesus made our relations with one another, especially the poor and needy, the sign of our relationship with God. The parable of the last judgment is very clear. According to the parable, all people will be separated according to whether they cared for those in need or not.

The King will say to those on his right: "Come, blessed of my Father! Take possession of the kingdom prepared for you from the beginning of the world. For I was hungry and you fed me, I was thirsty and you gave me drink. I was a stranger and you welcomed me into your house. I was naked and you clothed me. I was sick and you visited me. I was in prison and you came to see me." When they asked when they had seen God in need, the reply was straightforward: "Truly I say to you: whenever you did this to one of the least, of these my sisters and brothers, you did it to me" (Matthew 25:34-40).

How can you love God whom you do not see, if you do not love your neighbor, Jesus asked? But our neighbors can be very difficult to love. They can be demanding and insulting, unappreciative and destructive. They can make us very angry or feel burdened. For five years, I lived in an African township on the outskirts of Harare, the capital of Zimbabwe. Several houses away from us lived a large family with many problems. The father was a drunkard and gambler. He and his wife had eleven children. The wife brewed beer to support the children. As the children grew up, the firstborn was arrested for theft; another son was imprisoned for murder; the eldest daughter had three children out of wedlock with different men; and one of the younger daughters died having an abortion.

And yet this family was very lovable, and each member became a loyal friend and companion. The mother would confide in us about her marital problems and seek advice about birth control. When she fell pregnant in her late thirties with her twelfth child, she named her after me. The eldest son used to help us around the garden. He became our protector and kept thieves away from us. I found a job for the oldest girl as housemaid for one of my workmates and was disappointed when she ran away from the job to live with a married man.

Though we came from different cultures and different social classes, our proximity to one another bound us together. They taught us about the joys and hardships of life in a poor Shona family. We never doubted that they would protect us from danger and when they brought us a bunch of bananas from their tree or a dozen eggs, it was a precious gift, like the widow's mite in the Bible—giving all they had. We, in turn, could give them access to goods and services from which their poverty would exclude them, such as proper health care and education.

When I return to the States on my home leave every few years, I am always surprised to find that neighbors don't know one another and often don't even greet each other. Parishioners in large urban churches rush off after services, hardly pausing to nod or smile. I doubt if anyone could say of them, "See these Christians, how they love one another."

Perhaps the elephant can remind us that no matter how big and powerful we are, we still need each other. Life is less human and less pleasant when we put our independence and personal freedom ahead of community values and family ties. I once saw a herd of elephants mourn an elder who had died. They caressed his tusks with their trunks and processed solemnly around the fallen beast with heads bent low and ears flapping. They expressed their sorrow and loss as poignantly as any sorrowing widow.

Do we express our care and concern for one another? Do we let our personal schedules be upset by the needs of others or do we prefer our solitary splendor? Are we prepared to compromise our personal preferences to accommodate another? Do we truly believe that God is present in each person we meet? Can we communicate our deepest longings to another or do we stay locked up within ourselves?

Let us ask God to turn our hearts of stone into a heart of flesh. Let us learn to love our neighbors as ourselves.

Scripture

"This is my commandment: Love one another as I have loved you. There is no greater love than this, to give one's life for one's friends; and you are my friends if you do what I command you." (John 15:12-14)

"By this everyone will know that you are my disciples, if you have love for one another." (John 13:35)

"The whole community of believers were one in heart and mind. No one considered as his or her own what belonged to them; but rather they shared all things in common....There was no needy person among them, for those who owned land or houses sold them and brought the proceeds of the sale and laid it at the feet of the apostles who distributed it according to each one's need." (Acts 4:32-37)

Reflection

1. Who is your community?
2. How do you go about strengthening your relationships with others? In your family? In your neighborhood? In your workplace?
3. Are you involved in any projects to assist the needy members of the community?

Action

1. Let another person know how much you care about her/him this week.
2. Communicate with a friend or relative who is far away.

GIRAFFE

Adaptation and Flexibility

The world's tallest mammal, the giraffe, is the skyscraper of the savanna. An adult giraffe can grow eighteen feet tall and weigh up to four thousand pounds and yet is one of the most graceful animals on the plain. To watch a giraffe run at a gallop, forelegs and hind legs working in pairs like a running rabbit, is like watching a skilled ballerina leap across a stage. A giraffe has a huge heart in order to pump blood up its long neck to its head. To drink, a giraffe must either straddle or bend its forelegs. It has a very delicate mechanism that controls the flow of blood to the head to prevent it from fainting each time it bends down to drink. Supremely adapted to living in a harsh environment, the giraffe can eat thorny branches at the tops of trees where no other animal can reach. Its tongue grows up to eighteen inches long in order to get around the thorns to the nutritious leaves, and a modified atlas-axis joint lets it extend its head further to increase its height advantage. The only predator of an adult giraffe is the lion, but one swift kick from a grown giraffe can easily fell the king of the beasts.

As someone who has lived more than half of my life on the African continent, I have discovered the necessity of being adaptable and flexible. Sometimes crossing cultural barriers can be like trying to get past the thorns on the tree to find the

nourishing leaves. Faced with such strong cultural differences, even when I thought I was being patient and open, I discovered that others did not find me so. It is so easy to judge that which is different as inferior or wrong and to accept our own definition of reality as correct and normative for all time and all people.

I recall the first time that I visited a Maasai *boma* in rural Tanzania. The homes are rounded spheres, made of mud brick, with a low doorway that one must bend to enter. In Maasai culture, cows represent wealth. Their milk and blood provide food; their dung is used for a kind of cement that is smeared on the outside of the homes to offer protection against rain and wind; and their skin provides blankets on which to sleep and sit. At night the cows sleep in the center of the homestead, which causes swarms of flies. Inside the house, a fire is kept burning to produce smoke that keeps away the flies, but outdoors one learns to live with the constant companionship of flies sitting on lips, nose, and eyes. It is a true feat, one that could undo even the most stoic monk, to refrain from swatting the flies away from one's face. Yet, the Maasai seem not to notice these ever-present pests.

So far removed was this Maasai village from the lower-middle-class neighborhood where I grew up in Pittsburgh that I had no compass with which to adjust myself. I was thrown completely off balance and did not know what to do or how to respond. My eyes were smarting from the smoke, as I entered the home of one of the elders. His wife showed me the lattice work entrances to the sleeping shelves that are built into the wall. I wondered what it would be like to sleep there, on a hard mud slab with no soft sheets or warm blankets. I tasted the honey beer that had bees floating on top and even drank heated cow's blood. It all seemed very exotic and unreal. I wondered what they thought of me, an outsider who didn't speak their language, wore funny clothes, and drove in a Land Rover.

This village was part of a Christian community where Spiritan missioner Vincent Donovan and two Maryknoll Sisters, Julia Kubista and Ann Narciso, worked. They were attempting a unique inculturation experience—to accept the Maasai culture as it was and incorporate many of its elements into the Christian liturgy. Too often in the past, Christianity and Western culture were seen to be identical. When the Second Vatican Council (1963-1965) challenged this notion and encouraged cultural adaptation, the Holy Spirit missioners in East Africa were among the first to try to implement this within a specific culture, that of the Maasai.

The service began with a traditional dance and song of welcome. A Maasai ritual of forgiveness, in which a handful of grass is passed around the group, followed. Other traditional rituals were incorporated into the service, including a blessing of peace that involved a sprinkling with cow's milk. The children were the first to receive the Eucharist at this unique service, in keeping with the Maasai custom of feeding the children first so that they would have enough to eat even in times of scarcity and drought. Fr. Donovan explained that if the children were excluded from the sacrament, the Maasai would never accept it since the children are included in every part of their culture. As I observed this liturgy, the differences between us seemed to vanish and I experienced a oneness that transcended all boundaries.

After the service, the feeling of unity continued and I felt a genuine welcome to partake in a meal and to share some of the love of family and friends that I witnessed. I have rarely seen a people so proud of themselves and their culture; a people who walk tall and refuse to adopt Western culture even in the externals. I went away with a deep admiration for these rare people, and a deep sadness, knowing that one day they too would be forced to lose much of what they value as the "modern world" moved in. I wonder if they will retain the core values of their culture as the externals change.

As the world is becoming increasingly globalized, we find we are rubbing shoulders with people of many diverse cultures. Our neighbors may be from Japan, China, Saudi Arabia, Ethiopia, Nigeria, or Iraq. Like the Maasai, all people are proud of their culture. Culture gives meaning to their lives and bestows a sense of identity. What will the effects of globalization mean to the original inhabitants of a place? When our neighbors come from different cultures, will we jump to conclusions and rely on stereotypes about them? Or can we, like the giraffe, learn to adapt to our environment, an environment that is becoming increasingly diverse and multicultural? Can we make conscious efforts to modify our thoughts and behavior to accept cultures that differ from ours? Can we overcome our fear to reach out in friendship to the stranger in our midst?

Scripture

"Do not judge and you will not be judged. In the same way you judge others, you will be judged, and the measure you use for others will be used for you. Why do you see the speck in your neighbor's eye and not see the plank in your own eye?" (Matthew 7:1-4)

"All were filled with the Holy Spirit and began to speak other languages, as the Spirit enabled them to speak. Staying in Jerusalem were religious Jews from every nation under heaven. When they heard this sound, a crowd gathered, all excited because each heard them speaking in their own language." (Acts 2:4-6)

"Peter stood up and said to them, 'Brothers, you know what God did among us in the early days, so that non-Jews could hear the Good News from me and believe. God, who can read hearts, put himself on their side by giving the Holy Spirit to them just as he did to us. God made no distinction between us and them and cleansed their hearts through faith. So why do you want to put God to the test? Why do you lay on the disciples a burden that neither our ancestors nor we ourselves were able to carry?'" (Acts 15:7-10)

Reflection

1. Have you ever felt like an outsider? How did you respond?
2. Have others ever questioned things you took for granted as correct and proper? How did this make you feel?
3. Have you experimented with new kinds of food from another culture? Have you learned another language? How did it feel to stretch yourself beyond your normal limits, to go outside your comfort zone?
4. Have you ever found yourself making negative or critical judgments of customs that are different from yours? How can you find out the meaning behind them?

5. Have you ever been afraid of a person from another culture just because that individual was different from you or because of negative generalizations that you had heard from others? How can you increase your knowledge and understanding of those who differ from you?

Action

1. Go to an ethnic restaurant and try food that you have never tasted before.
2. Read the Holy Book of another religion (the Qur'an, the Bible, and so on) and share what you learned with a friend.
3. Attend a prayer service of a religious group not your own.
4. Learn a new language.

GREATER KUDU

Freedom

The kudu stands erect and majestic, like a king surveying its territory. With long spiral horns that can grow to seventy-two inches in length, a slender body, and a reddish-brown coat marked with distinctive white stripes, the kudu is the second tallest member of the antelope family.

Found throughout eastern and southern Africa, these gourmet browsers thrive on 118 different kinds of leaves, herbs, fruits, tubers, succulents, and flowers. The males associate in transient bachelor herds of ten to twenty animals, roaming over vast expanses of wood and grassland, while exclusive and long-lasting associations between females set them apart from other antelopes. Their smaller relatives, the lesser kudu, are simply miniature versions of their tall and stately cousins.

When threatened, kudu either sneak away without being seen or take flight, easily leaping over obstacles eight feet high. Watching a kudu in flight is like watching a high-jumper clear hurdles in long, graceful strides, without a pause to reposition or gain leverage. A kudu once leaped over the hood of a car I was driving near Victoria Falls. My spirit soared with it, although my heart was beating fast as I wondered what would have happened if it had missed and all five hundred pounds or more had come crashing down on me!

Whether standing still or in flight, the kudu exudes a sense of power and invincibility. One feels a kind of freedom in its presence. Some people exude a similar sense of inner strength and freedom. Ironically, it is often people who have been oppressed who emerge stronger and more self-reliant from their experience of suffering. Nelson Mandela readily comes to mind as someone who overcame difficulties to reach a self-awareness and self-acceptance that enabled him to forgive his former enemies and build a multiracial society on the foundation of a deeply divided nation. Truly a modern-day miracle!

A lack of freedom stunts and cripples people, making it difficult for them to have hopes and dreams for their lives. It robs them of confidence and makes them feel inferior. I saw this when I arrived in what was then Rhodesia in 1977 at the height of the liberation war. The segregation there, similar to South Africa under apartheid and the United States before the civil rights movement, effectively kept people of different races apart. Worse than that, it excluded people because of the color of their skin from basic rights such as good jobs, education, and health care.

I was present when Rhodesia became Zimbabwe on April 18, 1980. Almost overnight, things began to change in this former British colony. Black children could now attend good schools that had been reserved exclusively for whites. Blacks could now receive treatment at government clinics and hospitals that had previously been for whites only. Not only was the African population able to gain access to resources and facilities previously denied them, but, more importantly, they now felt good about themselves. There was a spring to their step, a light in their eyes, and a smile on their faces that was contagious.

Mr. Madimbizi, a dignified elderly gentleman in our local parish, was a gardener in the home of a wealthy white family. He told me how independence changed his life. "They always called me boy," he said. In colonial Rhodesia, servants were commonly known as "boy" no matter what their age—there were garden boys, kitchen boys, and house boys. "I told them I am Mr. Madimbizi," he said, with pride. "That is my name. I am the son of Chinamora, husband of Ruth Farai, and father of Amos and Tendai." What a small but significant change! Like the kudu, he now stood tall and majestic, having surmounted a barrier to equality and human dignity.

This transformation also liberated his employers. For the first time perhaps, they realized that he was an adult like them, with similar hopes and dreams for his family. They began to treat him differently, with the respect due another human being. The African concept of *ubuntu* captures the reality that we are all children of God, created in God's likeness. Bishop Desmond Tutu describes it like this:

> In Africa recognition of our interdependence is called *ubuntu*. . . . It is the essence of being human. It speaks of the fact that my humanity is caught up and inextricably bound up in yours. I am human because I belong. It speaks about wholeness; it speaks about compassion. . . .
>
> All South Africans were less whole than we would have been without apartheid. Those whites who were privileged lost out as they became more uncaring, less compassionate, less humane, and therefore less human. . . .*

They needed to be freed from the oppression of their privilege. What an amazing concept!

The story of the exodus in the Old Testament is a powerful testimony of God's intervention in history to free the oppressed. Zimbabwean refugees in the camps in Mozambique told me often how this story gave them hope and courage. "God led the people of Israel across the Red Sea to the Promised Land. God will also lead us to freedom," they said.

In the New Testament, Jesus tells us that there is need to be liberated from sin as well as from external bondage. When he forgave sin as part of his healing ministry, he demonstrated that inner freedom is as important as outer freedom. "What good is it to gain the

---

* Desmond Tutu, *God Has A Dream: A Vision of Hope for Our Time* (New York: Doubleday/Image, 2005), 26, 51.

whole world but destroy yourself?" Jesus asked (Mark 8:36). This is meant to be a wake-up call for those who are so busy acquiring personal wealth and power that they overlook their own need for salvation and the needs of their neighbor—the starving, homeless, sick, and helpless in our own backyard and around the world. As Christians, we are called like Moses to help liberate others. It can be as simple as calling someone by their name.

Scripture

"Yahweh said, 'I have seen the humiliation of my people in Egypt and I hear their cry when they are cruelly treated by their taskmasters. I know their suffering. I have come down to free them from the power of the Egyptians and to bring them up from that land to a beautiful spacious land, a land flowing with milk and honey. Go now! I am sending you to Pharaoh to bring my people, the sons and daughters of Israel, out of Egypt.'" (Exodus 3:7-10)

"Now, in Christ Jesus, all of you are sons and daughters of God through faith. All of you who were given to Christ through baptism, have put on Christ. Here there is no longer any difference between Jew or Greek, nor between slave and freedman, or between man and woman: but all of you are one in Christ Jesus. And because you belong to Christ, you are of Abraham's race and you are to inherit God's promise." (Galatians 3:26-29)

"For in Christ we obtain freedom, sealed by his blood, and have the forgiveness of sins. In this appears the greatness of his grace, which he lavished on us." (Ephesians 1:7-8)

Reflection

1. Have you ever experienced a lack of freedom in your life? How did it feel? What did you do?
2. Do you know others who are oppressed in some way? How can you help to liberate them?
3. Are you aware of the privileges that you enjoy based solely on your race or gender? How does this make you feel? What can you do to overcome this and relate as equals to those less privileged?

Action

1. Join a program in your community to help immigrants learn to read and write.
2. View the Web page of the Maryknoll Office for Global Concerns (www.maryknoll ogc.org) to learn about modern-day oppression worldwide. Find out what you can do to bring hope and freedom to others.

HAMMERKOP

Ambition

Weighing just a little more than a pound, the hammerhead, or hammerkop as it is called in Afrikaans, builds huge nests that may reach 110 pounds. The nests can be six feet tall and some are strong enough to support the weight of a person. One sees these large structures made of grass, reeds, sticks, and other local materials wedged in the fork of trees or perched on rocky ledges near water. Brown in color, the hammerkop's crested head is shaped like a hammer, hence its name. The hammerkop lives near streams, rivers, and lakes throughout sub-Saharan Africa and dines on small fish, frogs, tadpoles, insects, and other aquatic treats.

Abandoned nests are soon claimed by owls, bees, geese, snakes, and other animals or birds that benefit from the hammerkop's largesse. It is natural to wonder why such a small bird builds such a large house. Perhaps it simply enjoys the creative work of construction or maybe the largest nest attracts the strongest and most prolific mate.

I suspect that the hammerkop's ambitious building project reaps some unknown rewards. Among humans, ambition is often considered a negative trait that is frowned upon. "You're very ambitious, aren't you?" is a classic putdown when someone tries to achieve an impressive goal or is selected for a leadership position that another may have coveted.

Without ambition, however, we would not have Olympic athletes or renowned artists, dancers, or musicians. Extraordinary structures such as the pyramids, the Taj Mahal, Machu Picchu or the stone ruins of Great Zimbabwe might never have been built, and great feats such as climbing Mount Kilimanjaro or exploring the seas might never have been attempted.

Slavery might still be widespread without the ambitious aim of the abolitionists, and women would remain second-class citizens (as indeed they still are in many parts of the world) without the tireless advocacy of the suffragists and the women's movement. Without the dream of Martin Luther King Jr. and the civil rights activists who joined him, segregation might still exist in the United States. Without Nelson Mandela and the anti-apartheid movement that supported him, South Africa might still be in the grip of gross inequality based on race alone.

Healthy ambition enables us to go beyond the ordinary and the routine to accomplish wonders. *Ordinary People, Extraordinary Deeds* is the title of a recent film about the Maryknoll Sisters. It shows us working with disadvantaged people around the world, affirming the dignity of each person and lighting fires of hope in people's hearts.

Ambition leads to dreams and to small miracles. I have seen so many during my lifetime that I have lost count! Judy Mayotte, a friend of mine, lived among the displaced and uprooted peoples of the world for two years. Khmer refugees on the Thai-Cambodia border, Afghan refugees in Pakistan, and Eritrean and internally displaced Sudanese in Sudan became her family. She stayed in their makeshift homes, shared their food, ran with them to escape shelling, and listened to their stories, which she wrote about in *Disposable People: The Plight of Refugees* (Orbis Books, 1992). In 1993 when she returned to Sudan on a mission for Refugees International, she was seriously injured during an air drop of food aid that went amiss.

After her crushed leg was amputated just below the knee and she was no longer able to travel in war zones, she became a special adviser to the Clinton administration on refugee issues. She continues to teach on refugee and human rights issues and has established international learning programs for students at Seattle and Marquette Universities to help a new generation become more engaged, responsible global citizens. Judy now lives in Cape Town, South Africa, where she works with the Desmond Tutu Peace Centre and teaches at the University of the Western Cape.

Judy has never allowed her missing limb to define her or limit her dreams. She has accomplished more than most people with two legs and has not been deterred by the physical challenges she faces each day as she moves about in a wheelchair. This kind of ambition enables one to overcome difficulties, to touch many people's lives and to have a positive impact on the wider world.

Jesus expected similar achievements from his disciples. He commissioned them to go out in pairs to preach the gospel to a largely hostile audience, and he instructed them to travel lightly. "He ordered them to take nothing for the journey except a staff; no food, no bag, nor money in their belts. They were to wear sandals and were not to take an extra tunic" (Mark 6:8-9).

They were also told that they could perform miracles if they had faith. "If only you had faith the size of a mustard seed, you could tell that mountain to move from here to there, and the mountain would obey. Nothing would be impossible to you" (Matthew 17:20).

Like the hammerkop and witnesses like Judy Mayotte, we can go beyond the expectations that others might have of us. We can overcome the limitations of age or gender or of limited physical and mental abilities. We too can perform wonders if we only have faith!

Scripture

"Truly, I say to you: if you had faith and did not doubt, not only could you do what I have done with the fig tree, but you could even say to that mountain: 'Go and throw yourself into the sea!' and it would be done. Whatever you ask for in prayer full of faith, you will receive." (Matthew 21:21-22)

"I came weak, fearful and trembling: my words and preaching were not brilliant or clever to win listeners. It was, rather, a demonstration of spirit and power, so that your faith might be a matter not of human wisdom but of God's power." (1 Corinthians 2:3-5)

"Gladly, then, will I boast of my weakness that the strength of Christ may be mine. So I rejoice when I suffer infirmities, humiliations, want, persecutions: all for Christ! For when I am weak, then I am strong." (2 Corinthians 12:9-10)

Reflection

1. Have you overcome a personal difficulty to achieve a goal that meant a lot to you? When? How?

2. What are the causes or needs that inspire you to go beyond your normal capacity to achieve a victory?

Action

1. Join others working to achieve positive change in an area that matters to you.
2. Assist in a program for those with physical or mental disabilities, helping them to believe in themselves and accomplish their dreams.

HIPPOPOTAMUS

Humility and Self-Acceptance

A myth of the San people, a tribe of southern Africa, says that the hippopotamus was one of the last creatures God made and so God used bits and pieces that were left over from others. Ashamed that he was so fat and ugly, the hippo begged God to let him live in the water so that no one would see him. God refused: with such a large mouth and teeth, he would devour too many fish. Hippo promised he would not eat the fish but would graze on grass. God finally agreed. Hippos come out of the water at night to graze when no one can see them and spend most of their days in the water. The San people believe that when hippos defecate, they brush the dung with their tails so that God can examine it and be sure that there are no fish bones.

often wish that I were a combination of Mother Teresa, Dorothy Day, and Thomas Merton. The San myth reminds me that God expects me to be myself and to develop my own type of spirituality rather than trying to imitate others. Mary Josephine (Mollie) Rogers, the foundress of the Maryknoll Sisters, very wisely advised her members to use their own gifts—the unique gifts that God gave to each one—to attract others to God. She did not believe in a regimented form of religious life, where individuals conformed to a common model, losing their unique identity. In 1930 she wrote, "Each one of us, in her own work, with her own particular attractiveness is to be used by God as a particular tool to do a particular work and to save particular souls. That explains our spirit, an attempt to keep our individuality."

It is often easier to fit into a mold than to accept and develop one's own identity. Like the hippo, we can believe that we are too stupid or too weak or too fearful to be accepted and loved as we are. We can try to disguise our true selves and spend most of our lives running away from the truth. The current "self-help" craze sometimes overdoes the emphasis on finding self and being true to self, but without self-acceptance and self-love, we can do little for ourselves or for others.

"Love your neighbor as yourself," Jesus advises us. It is a false spirituality that tells us that it is selfish to love ourselves and that we must ever bow before the wishes of others. Such a spirituality encourages us to focus on our faults and mistakes rather than on our gifts and achievements. This is not the spirituality of Jesus and his disciples, who were unique human beings with all their weaknesses and foibles. Peter was arrogant and bold, yet Jesus made him the head of the church. John and his brother were greedy and wanted the first places in the kingdom, and yet John was the beloved disciple. Mary was chastised by her sister, Martha, for being lazy and failing to do her share of the domestic duties, but Jesus praised her for "choosing the better part."

None of us is perfect. God uses our imperfections to make us more compassionate. "God writes straight with crooked lines," it has been said. The spiritual writer Henri Nouwen labels all God's followers "wounded healers." When we recognize and accept our own woundedness, we can accept the quirks and limitations of others. When we face the truth, however painful, we are offered the possibility of healing and redemption.

"It comes to me vividly as I place a fragment of broken bread into your outstretched hands and say 'the body of Christ,'" writes Simon Bailey, an Anglican priest who died of AIDS.

> These are infected hands, fingers, doing the distributing—not contagious and yet infected with a life-threatening, a body-threatening virus. And what I place in your hands is, I say also, a broken, crumbling, fragmented body for you to share in. As you share in the wide-open brokenness of Christ's body, his blood, his heart, you share in my destruction too—and in my reconstruction, in my healing, because my body is healed, eased, soothed by knowing that you share my pain.*

What a shocking, liberating insight! Never has the Eucharist made more sense to me. None of us is whole; each of us is hurting, scarred, beaten, and broken. In the awareness and acceptance of this reality, we embrace the reality of Christ's sacrifice and our role in the redemptive mystery. Yes, the body of Christ has AIDS. The body of Christ is healed. The body of Christ, your body, my body, is risen. Alleluia.

Scripture

> "O God, you search me and you know me.... It was you who formed my inmost parts and knit me together in my mother's womb.... Even my bones were known

---

* Simon Bailey, *The Well Within: Parables for Living and Dying* (London: Darton, Longman & Todd, 1996), 76-77.

to you when I was being formed in secret, fashioned in the depths of the earth." (Psalm 139:1, 13, 15)

"Do you not know that your body is a temple of the Holy Spirit within you, given by God?" (1 Corinthians 6:19)

Reflection

1. What are the weaknesses and imperfections that you try to hide from others? How would your life be different if you could embrace and accept them?
2. What do you find difficult to love and accept in others? Could this be a reflection of the part of yourself that you reject?
3. Can you recall examples from the Bible of the limitations and imperfections of God's chosen people in the Old Testament and the followers of Jesus in the New? What is God saying to us by these examples?

Action

1. Write your own Psalm 139, describing all the gifts and abilities that God has given you, as well as the weaknesses and limitations that are part of who you are.
2. Give an honest compliment to someone who generally annoys you.

HORNBILL

Unconditional Love

The distinctive curved beak of the hornbill is more than a decorative accessory. In hues of brilliant orange, red, and yellow, the beak of the male bird feeds his mate and their offspring during the month-long period when she is incubating her eggs and for several months after the eggs hatch. In order to protect the expectant mother and the infant birds from predators, the hornbill seals his mate within a hollow tree trunk, leaving only a small opening through which he feeds her several times a day. If he fails to return, his mate and offspring will starve to death in their wooden tomb. So faithful and devoted is the male that he is often referred to as a love bird and is sometimes captured, killed, and made into a "love potion" intended to promote fidelity and dedication in marriage or friendship.

When I was growing up in Pittsburgh, a young couple lived in the apartment above us. Their daughter, Barbie, was a few years younger than I. We soon became fast friends even though she was a "pedestrian," my eight-year-old version of Presbyterian. In those days before the Catholic Church encouraged ecumenism, interreligious friendships were discouraged.

A few years after they moved to our neighborhood, Barbie's mother developed tuberculosis and was taken to a sanatorium to recover. When she was released several months later, she was very weak and frail and could no longer do much of the house-work or cooking. Her husband, Bill, worked the night shift in the police force. By day he cooked, cleaned, and looked after his wife and daughter. He could not have had more than a few hours of sleep a day, but Bill was such a devoted husband and father that he considered no sacrifice too great to preserve the health of his wife and to nourish the growth of his beautiful daughter.

Bill was a tough police officer and I would not have wanted to be the criminal who fell into his hands. But with his family, he was the most gentle and considerate person I have ever met. His wife and daughter knew that they were precious in his eyes and they repaid him with undying love. They trusted him to provide everything they needed. Like the female hornbill, they did not doubt that he would faithfully care for them.

I imagine that God's love, like Bill's and that of the hornbill, is total, unending, with-out measure. It is the lifeblood flowing through us, the song in our voices, the dance in our steps, the inner strength that enables us to survive the hard knocks and disappoint-ments that are part of life.

In 1977, I was sent to Rhodesia from Kenya to be the press secretary for the Catho-lic Commission for Justice and Peace. After only three months of documenting the atrocities of the colonial army against civilians, the government swooped down on our office, arresting me and several others, claiming that our reports were causing "alarm and despondency," a crime under the regime of Ian Smith. I was detained in Chikurubi Prison for three weeks before being deported. Those three weeks were the best retreat I ever made.

As I read the Psalms and the Gospels in my prison cell, I felt that they were written just for me. Each stanza and verse spoke of God's love and protection in time of trial. I wrote in my diary that "I knew that God was with me in my prison cell." Even though the bed was filthy and full of lumps, the food tasteless, the routine and lack of freedom monotonous and the uncertainty about the future frightening, I have never felt so peaceful and contented in my life. God's love became as real as the air I breathed and the blood that coursed through my veins. It was the sweetest comfort that I have ever known, before or since.

We do not have to be arrested and imprisoned to experience God's love, nor does God speak to us only when we are in trouble and suffering. God tells us that divine love is like that of a mother hen gathering her chicks under her wing, or a shepherd who goes searching for the one sheep that is lost, or the woman who sweeps her house looking for the lost coin. God is never far from us.

We can count on God's love and protection every moment of our lives. Like the female hornbill imprisoned in the tree, we can depend on God never to abandon us, no matter how far we stray from God. God asks only that we love others in return.

Scripture

"The love of God has been poured into our hearts.... But see how God manifested his love for us: while we were still sinners, Christ died for us and we have become just through his blood." (Romans 5:5-8)

"This is love: not that we loved God but that he first loved us and sent his Son as an atoning sacrifice for our sins.... God is love. Those who live in love, live in God and God in them." (1 John 4:10, 16)

"Now I give you a new commandment: love one another. Just as I have loved you, you also must love one another. By this everyone will know that you are my disciples, if you have love for one another." (John 13:34-35)

Reflection

1. Do you know anyone as dedicated and self-sacrificing as the hornbill?
2. Have you ever been this devoted to another person?

3. When have you experienced the unselfish devoted love of another? Of God?
4. When have you given total love without counting the cost?

Action

1. Write your own psalm of God's love.
2. Show a friend or family member that you care about her or him by doing something special for that person.

IMPALA

Openness to Change

A unique antelope, with no known close relatives, impala live in large herds throughout the southern savanna, from central Kenya to northern South Africa and westward through Angola and Namibia. Small and graceful, they resemble the gazelle in size and coloring, but belong to a different species.

Impala outnumber other antelope on the African plain because of their openness to accept change. They frequently change their diet, for instance, depending on their location and the season of the year. During the rainy season, they subsist on grass, and when the dry season comes, they switch to leaves, herbs, shoots, and seedpods. This ability to be both grazer and browser enables them to thrive in almost any habitat. They can also survive without drinking for long periods although they usually live near water.

Impala have a unique way of escaping predators. When sensing danger, they scatter in all directions, making tremendous leaps into the air, as much as ten feet high and thirty-six feet long, confusing their attackers and losing them in the chase.

While female impala live together in large herds, offering many opportunities for males to mate, the males live in bachelor herds and compete for mating rights. Only the dominant male in a territory gets to reproduce, but after three months he usually tires of guarding his harem against interlopers and is replaced. Forced out by a rival, he joins another herd until he is strong enough to compete again. These frequent changes of location prevent inbreeding and keep the herd strong.

Unlike the impala, we humans often find it difficult to accept change. We easily become accustomed to our habits and our way of life. Changing neighborhoods, jobs, or even diet can be a major challenge to us. We take the same route to work every day, sit in the same pew at church every week, and follow the same schedule from year to year.

While this regularity has the advantage of making life more secure and predictable, there is the danger that it will extend to more critical areas of our lives, making us unable to adjust to new realities and intolerant of those who differ from us. We may find it hard to let go of assumptions and prejudices, for example, and may cling to our views even when there is no evidence to support them.

The Shona people of Zimbabwe have many names for God. My favorite is *Chipindikure*, "the One who turns things upside down." It comes from the root *kupinduka*, which means to be uprooted. What an amazing concept to explain God's presence in the often unwanted and unplanned changes that happen to us throughout our lives! These can bring many blessings if we are open to the invitation to change, or they can make us miserable if we resist.

My own life has been full of such invitations. I was very happy and fulfilled in my first mission in Nairobi, Kenya, where I headed the communications office of the Catholic Church. Training local journalists and broadcasters was a very rewarding profession, and my community was very open and caring. I had no desire to leave Nairobi or change jobs.

But on my birthday in 1977 (February 13), I received a totally unexpected invitation to be the press secretary of the Catholic Commission for Justice and Peace in Rhodesia. Rhodesia was then in the midst of a brutal war for independence, and the Commission was known for its outspoken criticism of white minority rule. I knew instantly that this was where God was calling me, although it meant leaving behind so much that I had grown to love.

I made the change by the end of May that year. After documenting the war crimes of the Ian Smith army for three months, I had another unexpected call to change. As I noted above in my reflection on the hornbill, I was arrested, detained for three weeks, and then deported back to the United States. This very abrupt and unsettling experience helped to prepare me for other, less dramatic changes that lay ahead. A year later, I responded to a call to work with Zimbabwean refugees in Mozambique, which led to a new ministry in the field of education, development, and leadership training.

Each of these changes was completely unexpected and very demanding, and yet each brought me new life and energy. Truly, I had been turned upside down and forced to let go of much that I had enjoyed and valued. The most recent call to change came in October 2008, when I was elected to leadership in my community. Called to leave Zimbabwe, a country that had been home to me for almost thirty years, I embarked on a new adventure. I have learned to be both a browser and a grazer and have never regretted the unsettling and transforming response to God's unexpected calls.

Scripture

"As Jesus was walking along the shore of Lake Galilee, he saw Simon and his brother Andrew casting a net in the lake, for they were fishermen. And Jesus said to them, 'Follow me, and I will make you fishers of men.' At once, they left their nets and followed him." (Mark 1:16-18)

"As Saul traveled along and was approaching Damascus, a light from the sky suddenly flashed around him. He fell to the ground and heard a voice saying to him, 'Saul, Saul! Why do you persecute me?' And he asked, 'Who are you, Lord?' The voice replied, 'I am Jesus whom you are persecuting. Now get up and go into the city; there you will be told what you are to do.'" (Acts 9:3-6)

"After living in Moab for about ten years . . . Naomi was left bereft of husband and two sons. Having heard that Yahweh had come to help his people by giving them food, Naomi prepared to return home. With her two daughters-in-law, she took the road back to Judah. It was then that Naomi said to her daughters-in-law, 'Go back, each of you to your mother's house. . . .' Ruth replied, 'Don't ask me to leave you. For I will go where you go and stay where you stay. Your people will be my people and your god my God. Where you die, there will I die and be buried.'" (Ruth 1:5-8, 16-17)

Reflection

1. Have you responded to an invitation that changed your life? How did it happen? What did you do?
2. How do you determine what to retain and what to change in your life?

Action

1. Try something new. It could be something very ordinary such as trying out a new recipe or something more demanding such as helping out at a food pantry or a homeless shelter or taking in a foster child.
2. Ask yourself how you can respond to invitations to help that you may see in newspapers or on the Internet. Maryknoll's Web site (www.maryknoll.org) offers many opportunities to help that will bring change to your life and to the lives of others.

LION

Playfulness and Leisure

Lions are big, strong, and dangerous, feared by animals and humans alike. Aptly called the "king of the beasts," the lion has few equals when it comes to hunting prowess and survival skills. The film Lion King *helped to immortalize the leadership and human qualities of this amazing animal. Although fiction, the film captured some of the dynamics that take place within the extended lion family. Rivalries, power struggles, and violence are commonplace between adult males who compete to control a pride of lions.*

Prides consist of several females and their offspring. A typical pride numbers about thirteen members, residing in a home range or territory that can be as small as eight square miles or as large as 154 square miles, depending on the availability of prey. Male offspring are forced to leave when they reach two and a half years, but prides of related females often live in the same home range, interacting with one another and sharing the same males, a kind of harem for the dominant males.

If you've ever watched a pride of lions relaxing in the shade of a thorn tree, cubs tumbling over one another while mothers nap nearby and father watches regally from a nearby rock, you might easily forget the danger and want to get closer and pet them as you would a domesticated cat. The antics of the baby lion in the *Lion King*, romping

with his friends, the warthog and the weasel, singing *Hakuna matata*—no problems, no trouble—portrays the playful side of this powerful beast. Adult males never lose their sense of play. Where prey is plentiful, lions can spend twenty out of twenty-four hours resting and playing, only going out to hunt in late afternoons or early evening.

In the modern, industrialized world, leisure time has become a scarce commodity, and recreation often means sitting in front of the television or the computer screen. Entertainment has become big business and costs big bucks. People often work weekends and take work home with them, only taking time out for the annual two-week holiday with their families. Is it any wonder that so many marriages end in divorce when so little time is spent relaxing together?

The church too has a tendency to equate hard work with goodness. When I joined religious life in the 1960s, most of our time was spent in manual labor or in the chapel. Only one hour was set aside each evening for community recreation. After the Second Vatican Council, rigid schedules and a regimented lifestyle were replaced with more flexibility. Instead of being ruled by the superior, however, many of us became ruled by our work. Now we may not even spare one hour a day to relax and enjoy one another's company, as we struggle to finish a funding proposal late at night or prepare for tomorrow's classes in the solitude of our room. Community life may mean no more than living under the same roof.

The fact that Jesus performed his first miracle at a wedding feast may offer a hint that he took fun and leisure seriously. One can imagine Jesus and his mother joining in the festivities with the other guests. Jesus took time to be with friends, enjoying meals at the home of Martha, Mary, and Lazarus and relaxing with them. When Martha chided her sister to come and help in the kitchen, Jesus gently reminded Martha that it was all right to take time off to converse with friends.

The creation story reminds us that God took a day off to sit back and enjoy creation, the origin of the Jewish Sabbath, when no work was to be done. It seems as if the heresy called Jansenism has joined hands with a puritanical work ethic to distort the lives of many modern Christians. Jansenism taught that enjoyment was sinful and that we were created to toil and sweat for our living. Doing good works became synonymous with sanctity. "Idle hands are the devil's workshop" is a saying I learned when I was very young. I still feel guilty when I take time off and I find myself needing to make excuses when I go on a holiday.

I marvel at my Zimbabwean friends who can spend the day laughing and talking to one another, even though they barely have enough to eat. No matter how difficult the living conditions, I find people singing, dancing, and praying. There is a tendency for Westerners to call this "laziness" and to condemn African societies to perpetual poverty because they refuse to adopt a Western work ethic. I believe that it is the other way around—that if the West would adopt the African play ethic and give priority to relationships, it would become more human in the process and there might be fewer heart attacks and less high blood pressure.

When I lived in refugee camps in Mozambique during Zimbabwe's liberation war, I was happily surprised to find that sport, drama, storytelling, song, and dance were an integral part of the timetable. It was called "raising morale." Cultural festivals were held at regular intervals so that people could develop their talents and entertain one another. Even though there was little food and few material resources, people found enjoyment and pleasure in one another's company and in entertaining one another with their God-given talents and creativity. How wonderful if we could all learn to slow down, stop looking at the clock and enjoy each other's company!

Lions are the only cats that hunt together. Perhaps they can cooperate in the hunt because they play together.

Scripture

"'Let the children come to me and don't stop them, for the kingdom of God belongs to such as these. Truly, I say to you, whoever does not receive the kingdom of God like a child will not enter it.' Then he took the children in his arms and laying his hands on them, blessed them." (Mark 10:14-16)

"The disciples came to Jesus and asked him, 'Who is the greatest in the kingdom of heaven?' Then Jesus called a little child, set the child in the midst of the disciples, and said, 'I assure you that unless you change and become like little children, you cannot enter the kingdom of heaven.'" (Matthew 18:1-5)

"Three days later there was a wedding at Cana in Galilee and the mother of Jesus was there. Jesus was also invited to the wedding with his disciples." (John 2:1-11)

Reflection

1. How do you usually spend your weekends?
2. Do you take work home with you to do in the evenings and on weekends?

3. What do you do to relax?
4. Can you remember what it was like to be a child? How have you changed? How can you recover some of your playfulness?

Action

1. Make the Sabbath holy by refraining from all work-related activity, including reading work-related material.
2. Take a picnic and go off to a quiet place with friends at least once a month.
3. Adopt a hobby such as bird watching, playing a musical instrument, jewelry making, pottery, or the like.
4. Take off your watch one day a week and don't look at a clock.

OSTRICH

Caution

The film Fantasia *has immortalized the ostrich as a graceful dancer, leaping through the air in a kind of synchronized ballet. The world's largest bird, standing nine feet tall, the ostrich actually does leap through the air in strides of up to sixteen feet. Unable to fly, it can sprint up to forty-three miles an hour. The ostrich's strong legs, which enable it to outrun predators, also serve as weapons. One swift kick can fell a lion.*

Human predators are not so easily defeated. The bird almost became extinct in the eighteenth century when its beautiful plumes were popular in ladies' fashions. They were also popular among African royal families, where they adorned headdresses and capes of paramount chiefs. Ostrich farming, which began in 1838, has preserved the ostrich, which is used for its feathers, meat, skin, and eggs.

The ostrich is a very sociable bird that lives in polygamous families of a dominant male, and a head female and her subordinates. Courtship is ritualized and synchronized, with graceful courting movements not unlike the Fantasia *dance. All females lay their eggs in the same nest, and the male plays a large part in constructing and guarding the nest as well as in raising the young.*

A large feathered bird with its head in the sand is another image commonly associated with the ostrich. It has come to represent those who live in denial, failing to face the problems of life. In fact, ostriches do not bury their heads in the sand, but when they sense trouble, they adopt a cautious posture, pressing their long necks to the ground in an attempt to become less visible. Their black, white, and brown feathers blend well with the sandy soil, enabling them to escape notice until the danger is past.

The cautionary approach of the ostrich is worth imitating in time of danger and distress. When I lived with refugees from Zimbabwe in the forests of Mozambique during Zimbabwe's liberation war, the refugees left the camps

at dawn each day to move several miles deeper into the trees in order to avoid aerial bombardment from what was then Rhodesia. They had learned to take this precaution from previous attacks when hundreds of men, women, and children were killed. Taking precautions in the face of danger is not cowardly; it is often the wisest thing we can do.

Wise parents caution their children against engaging in dangerous or illegal behavior such as taking alcohol and drugs or having premarital sex. Wise doctors counsel their patients to adopt healthy lifestyles, and wise pastors encourage their parishioners to do good and avoid evil.

Jesus urges us to exercise caution in the choices we make in our personal lives. He warns us not to store up treasures on earth that eventually disappear but to make choices that lead to eternal life. He asks the rich young man, for example, to share his possessions with the poor and needy. "Jesus looked steadily at him and loved him and he said, 'For you, one thing is lacking; go, sell what you have and give the money to the poor, and you will have riches in heaven. Then come and follow me'" (Mark 10:17-22). The young man bowed his head and turned away. He valued his possessions more than his relationship with Jesus.

In the Western world, it is normal to accumulate possessions. The entire advertising industry is intended to make us crave worldly goods. Consumption is portrayed as something positive. Each day we are bombarded with messages that entice us to buy the latest products, whether electronic gadgets, clothes, furniture, cars, toys, or whatever. Our closets bulge with unworn clothes, our garages overflow with lawn and garden products, our drawers are stuffed with things we rarely use. And yet, and yet—if we are asked to give some of our surplus to the poor, how do we react? Do we readily part with some of our excess or do we turn away sadly like the rich young man? His intentions were good but he lacked the will to sacrifice.

After almost forty years on the African continent, I still am amazed at how people survive with so little. A few cooking pots, a sleeping mat and a stool make up the worldly possessions of the majority of families. Each person might have two sets of clothing—one for work and one for Sundays and holidays. Running water, electricity, and indoor plumbing are amenities that most only dream of having; most people know that they will never enjoy these things in their lifetime despite all the political promises to the contrary. This abject material poverty is the other side of the coin to the overabundance in the North.

The imbalance in the use of the world's resources certainly calls for a word of caution. Distinguished world leaders such as Nelson Mandela, former president of South Africa, urge the rich "to live simply, so that others may simply live." Describing the inequality in the world as a new kind of apartheid, Mandela supports the "Live Simply Campaign" that was initiated several years ago by a group of Christian aid agencies to witness to the injustice in the world economic order and to try to address it. They remind us that violence grows from such gross inequality.

Stay awake! Be prepared! Live your life as if this might be the day of the Lord's coming, the Gospels urge us. Do we take time in our lives to step back and examine our choices? Do we know what we treasure? Are we aware of the part we play in maintaining the gap between the rich and the poor? Maybe it's time to stop, put our head to the ground to clear it of all distractions, and make good choices for the future.

Scripture

"Anyone who hears these words of mine and acts accordingly is like a wise person, who built a house on rock. The rain poured, the rivers flooded, and the wind blew and struck that house, but it did not collapse because it was built on rock. But anyone who hears these words of mine and does not act accordingly, is like a fool who built a house on sand. The rain poured, the rivers flooded, and the wind blew and struck that house; it collapsed and the ruin was complete." (Matthew 7:24-27)

"Do not store up treasure for yourself here on earth where moth and rust destroy it, and where thieves can steal it. Store up treasure for yourself with God, where no moth or rust can destroy nor thief come and steal it. For where your treasure is, there also your heart will be." (Matthew 6:19-21)

"Ten bridesmaids went out with their lamps to meet the bridegroom. Five of them were careless while the others were sensible. The careless bridesmaids took their lamps as they were and did not bring extra oil. But those who were sensible brought with their lamps flasks of oil." (Matthew 25:1-13)

Reflection

1. What guides the choices you make in your life?
2. Are you happy with your choices? Why or why not?
3. Do you take time to reflect on the direction your life is taking?

Action

1. The next time you have to make an important decision, stop and take time to think of the consequences of your choices.
2. Make time in your life for an annual retreat and for monthly days of recollection when you turn off the computer, radio, and television to reflect on the things that truly matter.
3. Look up information about the "Live Simply Campaign" on the Internet: www .livesimply.org.

OWL

Courage

Nocturnal birds of prey, owls fly noiselessly through the darkness, using their superior night vision and hearing to locate food. Of 132 species worldwide, 38 live on the African continent. The owl may locate a tree hole in which to lay its eggs or may take over the nests of other birds. Some owls perch on tree branches, remaining immobile during the day. An owl can twist its head almost 360 degrees, enabling it to spot prey in any direction. Rodents, birds, snakes, lizards, toads, fish, and insects are all part of the owl's diet.

The owl is generally viewed as an omen of bad luck throughout Africa. Sometimes associated with witchcraft, which is still prevalent in many parts of the continent, the owl is feared and avoided. Its hooting cry, sounding eerily through the darkness, and its silent approach make it a source of much folklore and myth.

When I first arrived in Africa, I had a tendency to equate such unscientific beliefs with superstition. Although I refuted the claims of earlier explorers and missioners that the African worldview was "primitive" or inferior, I soon realized that I shared some of these assumptions and prejudices myself.

Much later, when I was confronted with the experience of war, rape, torture, disappearance, and other forms of violence, I came in touch with my own insecurity and fear. As chair of a courageous team of doctors, nurses, counselors, and human rights activists who treated the victims of violence in Zimbabwe, I often feared the knock on the door in the middle of the night, signaling arrest, disappearance, beating, or death.

Some of my co-workers and friends had survived such trauma, returning to continue their heroic and dangerous work. Lovemore Madhuku, who heads the National Constitutional Assembly (NCA), an independent civic group that seeks constitutional change in Zimbabwe, was arrested, beaten, and tortured more than twenty times. Once he was kidnapped,

badly beaten, and left by the side of the road for dead. If a passing motorist had not seen him and taken him to a hospital, he would surely have perished.

"I soon found that I had crossed the threshold of fear in the sense that I became strong through resisting," he explained in an interview. "You cannot theorize about these things and say I can face the police. No, you just get involved and then you face the situation at the time. . . . My conviction that I am doing the right thing is my strongest weapon against fear. . . . There could be 99 against me. But then God always ensures that there is one person who will come and whisper that he believes that what I am doing is right."*

I personally experienced the truth of Madhuku's words when I was imprisoned in colonial Rhodesia for supporting majority rule and exposing the war crimes of Ian Smith's security forces. As I was being taken to court, another prisoner bent over as if to tie her shoe laces and whispered to me, "Not only the church supports you; the whole country supports you." These words of encouragement enabled me to face the judge and speak the truth with confidence.

As I stood in the packed courtroom, uncertain what fate awaited me, the words of the gospel flashed before me: "You will be brought to trial before rulers and kings because of me and you will witness to them. But when you are arrested, do not worry about what you are to say and how you are to say it; when the hour comes, you will be given what you are to say. For it is not you who will speak; but it will be the Spirit of your Father in you" (Matthew 10:18-20).

---

* Geoffrey Bould, ed., *Conscience Be My Guide: An Anthology of Prison Writings* (London: Zed Books, 2005), 170.

Without fear, I testified that I viewed the colonial system as unjust and that, indeed, I supported the cause of freedom. Accusing me of being "a self-confessed supporter of communism and a terrorist," the judge refused me bail and sent me back to prison. To my surprise, the prison guards applauded me, saying, "We almost clapped when you wouldn't call them [the freedom fighters] 'terrorists.'" They told me that they only took this job because they had to feed their children but they also supported majority rule.

From that time onward, they would communicate with me and bring me small treats such as a piece of fruit or a plate of *sadza*, a stiff maize meal porridge that is the staple food of Zimbabweans. The day that I was deported the other prisoners knew about it before I did. Mostly young women who were accused of feeding the "terrorists" or trying to cross the border to join them, they smuggled letters to me to give to Amnesty International. Their letters told of the harsh conditions they were undergoing in prison and the beating and torture that they had suffered when they were captured. The Catholic Commission for Justice and Peace took these letters and made sure that they reached Amnesty and were widely publicized.

Never again have I experienced such a sense of solidarity and support. The memory alone continues to give me courage, helping to cast out fear. May the owl remind us that our fears may be baseless and that our worst nightmares may turn out to be our best friends. What we don't understand and fear may teach us that we are stronger than we thought. If we unite with others for a just cause, we can gain strength from each other. As Lovemore Madhuku teaches, "We will not have success in one day. There will be setbacks. But we want to build a broad foundation of convinced people who take a conscious decision to take risks and overcome their fear."

Scripture

"Do not be afraid of those who kill the body, but not the person. Rather be afraid of those who can destroy both body and soul in hell. For only a few cents you can buy two sparrows, yet not one sparrow falls to the ground without your Father's consent. As for you, every hair of your head has been counted. So do not be afraid: you are worth much more than many sparrows." (Matthew 10:28-31)

"Then a storm gathered and it began to blow a gale. The waves spilled over into the boat so that it was soon filled with water. And Jesus was in the stern, asleep on the cushion. They woke him up and said, 'Master, don't you care if we sink?' As Jesus awoke, he rebuked the wind and ordered the sea, 'Quiet now! Be still!' The wind dropped and there was a great calm. Then Jesus said to them, 'Why are you so frightened? Do you still have no faith?'" (Mark 4:37-40)

"The angel came to her and said, 'Rejoice, full of grace, the Lord is with you.' Mary was troubled at these words, wondering what this greeting could mean. But the angel said, 'Do not fear, Mary, for God has looked kindly on you.'" (Luke 1:28-30)

Reflection

1. What frightens you?
2. What gives you courage?

3. Do you know a person like Lovemore Madhuku who has been persecuted for his or her beliefs yet has motivated others to join in a just cause?

Action

1. Read a story about the life of a saint or martyr to learn how the individual gained the courage to follow Jesus regardless of the personal cost.
2. Take a risk to do something in which you deeply believe though it might be dangerous to get involved.

PORCUPINE (CRESTED)

Justice

The southern African crested porcupine is covered in sharp quills that protect it from enemies. Some quills grow up to twelve inches long and can inflict fatal damage on predators. Porcupines do not shoot the quills, as once thought, but the quills easily detach and can lodge in the snout or body of another animal. Barbed at the tip, they are not easily removed and can cause infection and death.

Porcupines are nocturnal animals that eat roots, bark, crops, and fruit. They are not aggressive and do not seek to harm others. But when attacked they can defend themselves, charging backwards to inflict damage with their prickly spears. New quills grow in to replace those that are lost.

This unique defense system reminds me of the variety of ways that we protect ourselves and deter others from causing us harm. People in North America often turn to the law to defend themselves against predators and to obtain justice. Lawsuits have become endemic in the United States. Doctors are sued for malpractice; manufacturers have class action suits brought against them; marriage partners divorce each other in court; criminals are tried for crimes that range from petty theft to murder and, if found guilty, pay a fine or go to prison. In the case of misdemeanors or lesser offenses, those

found guilty may be assigned to some form of community service. There is hardly a case that cannot respond to some sort of legal solution.

This kind of legal system often satisfies the victim and brings a certain kind of justice to bear. But legal arguments rarely bring about understanding, forgiveness, reconciliation, and healing. The death penalty, in particular, may satisfy a desire for revenge on the part of the relatives of the victim but cannot bring peace of mind or replace the loved one who has been lost.

African society has its own forms of justice. In some cases, people resort to mob violence, especially in the case of petty theft, where a thief is often beaten to death if captured. In rural villages, elders or local leaders form a village court that hears all parties to a dispute, trying to reach a verdict that will be acceptable to all and that will restore the relationships that have been damaged or broken. This is necessary in close-knit rural communities, where people must work together if they are to survive the harsh conditions in which they live.

At a prayer session with a local spirit medium who is both priest and healer, I observed traditional wisdom on display. Several of those gathered for the morning ritual brought cases to be resolved through this ancient ceremony. Relying on his knowledge of the community and the local customs and rites, the spirit medium listened and then dispensed his verdict and ascribed a penalty to be paid. Not unlike the Catholic sacrament of penance, the ceremony involved confession, contrition, and an act of atonement. In most cases, it involved holding a communal feast where the injured would be appeased.

South Africa tried another form of setting things right when it established the Truth and Reconciliation Commission at the end of the apartheid era. Headed by Bishop

Desmond Tutu, the Commission was tasked with hearing hundreds of cases and granting amnesty to perpetrators who acknowledged their crime before the families of those they had wronged. While not a perfect model, this came closer to a form of restorative justice, which seeks to reconcile the two parties and repair their relationship.

Jesus gave us an example of an even more radical model. He showed that mercy is as important as justice and that repentance and forgiveness are always possible. When he forgave the woman caught in adultery, he pointed out that no one is completely innocent of sin. He treated the woman at the well with respect, although he knew that she had been married and divorced more than once. He called a tax collector to be among his disciples in spite of the reputation of this occupation as being corrupt. He praised Mary Magdalene for her loving act of washing his feet rather than condemning her for an imperfect life.

Imagine how different the world would be if we all had this attitude! Our quills would be used to protect rather than injure, and we would seek to understand and forgive rather than harm or punish. Bishop Tutu summed it up well when he said, "Forgiving means abandoning your right to pay back the perpetrator in his own coin, but it is a loss which liberates the victim."*

Scripture

"While Jesus was at table in Matthew's house, many tax collectors and other sinners joined Jesus and his disciples. When the Pharisees saw this they said to his disciples,

---

* Desmond Tutu, *No Future without Forgiveness* (New York: Doubleday/Image, 1999), 219.

'Why is it that your master eats with those sinners and tax collectors?' When Jesus heard this he said, 'Healthy people do not need a doctor, but sick people do. Go and find out what this means: What I want is mercy, not sacrifice. I did not come to call the righteous but sinners.'" (Matthew 9:10-13)

"Yahweh says, 'Yet even now, return to me with your whole heart, with fasting, weeping and mourning. Rend your heart, not your garment. Return to Yahweh, your God—gracious and compassionate.' Yahweh is slow to anger, full of kindness and he repents of having punished." (Joel 2:12-13)

"Her sins, her many sins, are forgiven because of her great love. But the one who is forgiven little, has little love." (Luke 7:47)

Reflection

1. How have you sought to obtain justice when you have been wronged? What did you gain from it? What did you lose?
2. Read the parable of the Prodigal Son (Luke 15:11-32) and reflect on the feelings and actions of the three main characters. Do you think justice has been done? Why or why not? Why did the father forgive his wayward son? What was the result of this act of mercy?

Action

1. Study the social teachings of your faith tradition to learn how they can contribute to creating a more just society.
2. Lobby against the death penalty in those states that still have it. See http://www.deathpenaltyinfo.org for information about the death penalty; currently thirty-six states plus the U.S. military still impose the death penalty.

RHINOCEROS

Stability

The rhino is a creature of habit that rarely moves outside his or her territory. The predictability of the rhino and its faithfulness to habit is one of the reasons that it has become an endangered species. Poachers, who kill rhinos for their tusks, which are used as medicine or aphrodisiacs in some cultures, can easily locate the rhino, since their habits and their habitat are well known and rarely change. Rhinos tend to be solitary as well, except when mating or caring for their young.

Often, in our leadership and peace-building courses at Silveira House in Harare, we use animal characters to portray human behavior. This method helps people to laugh at their foibles and takes some of the sting out of giving honest feedback. During these sessions, the rhinoceros is given as an example of stubbornness. A picture shows the rhino with its legs firmly planted on the ground, refusing to budge for anything or anyone. This portrayal may do injustice to the rhino. It is true that the rhino is big and solid and can block a path. Rather than a sign of stubbornness, however, we might view this as fidelity. Such faithfulness and stability are rare in today's society, where change and novelty are the norm. Living in the fast lane has become synonymous with mobility and success.

I grew up in an age when fidelity and stability were almost taken for granted. Divorce was rare, people stayed at the same job for a lifetime, and families tended to settle in the same neighborhoods where they had been raised. This has changed radically in the United States but is still true in some parts of the world.

When I joined Silveira House in 1998, for instance, I was happy to learn that most of the staff had been there for twenty years or more. The first to retire was a driver who had been with the center since its foundation, thirty-two years earlier. This kind of loyalty is becoming increasingly rare with the hardships of daily life leading people to look for greener pastures wherever they can find

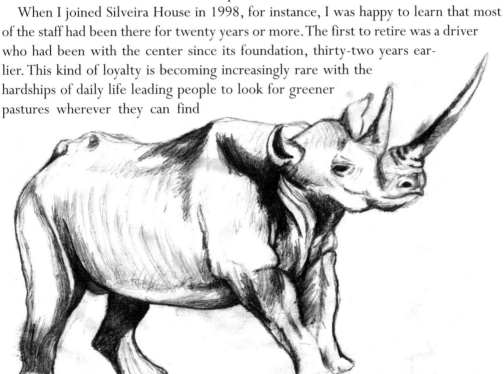

them. In the case of Zimbabweans, this may mean going to South Africa to look for temporary work or to engage in cross-border trading.

Jimmy made a very different choice. Although he had lived on the streets of Harare for eight years, Jimmy did not despair or turn to a life of crime, drugs, or alcohol, as is the case with many homeless youth. Instead, with the help of the St. Vincent de Paul Society at the cathedral parish, he did a four-month course in brick-laying at Silveira House. On completing his course, Jimmy got a job with a local construction company and was able to rent a room with his first month's salary. His life continued to improve. A few years later he married and built his own home. He named his first son Spence after the Jesuit priest who had helped him, and he became an active member of the St. Vincent de Paul Society, the group that had raised the funds for his course in masonry.

Now he is self-employed and spends his free time assisting those who are poor and homeless, as he had once been. I marveled that he was able to overcome his painful past, and asked him how he had managed to rebuild his life. "Fr. Spence counseled me," he explained. "He spent a day with me every week, teaching me the right way to live. When I did wrong, he corrected me. That's how I survived the tough life of the streets and changed my life for the better."

The advice and good example of a caring priest brought stability and a sense of purpose to Jimmy's life. One doesn't need a degree in counseling to be a mentor and guide to another. A willingness to take time and to listen is probably the major prerequisite. I was fortunate to have many wisdom figures in my life, especially some of our senior sisters who took time to listen to my hopes and dreams and to share with me the lessons they had learned through years of loving service in "fields afar." I treasure the hours I spent with them and try to follow their example in my own encounters with others who need a listening ear and an open heart.

"Am I my brother's keeper?" asked Cain, after killing his brother, Abel. God punished him for this act. In the New Testament, Jesus makes it very clear that we are meant to care for one another. The parable of the Good Samaritan takes this message one step further. We are expected to care not only for our friends and relatives but also for the stranger. Even more shocking is the knowledge that we are expected to care for and love our enemies.

Imagine what a different world it would be if we took this message seriously! How many Jimmys are waiting for a Samaritan to bind up their wounds, bring stability to their lives, and help them to start over?

Scripture

"What do you think someone does who has a hundred sheep and one of them gets lost? That person will leave the other ninety-nine grazing on the hillside and go and look for the lost sheep. When it is found, I tell you, one feels far happier over this one sheep than over the ninety-nine that did not get lost. In just the same way your Father in heaven does not want any of these little ones to be lost." (Matthew 18:12-15)

"Be on watch, be alert, for you do not know when the time will come. . . . Be on guard, then, because you do not know when the master of the house is coming—it might be in the evening or at midnight or before dawn or at sunrise. If the master comes suddenly, he must not find you asleep. What I say to you, then, I say to all: Watch!" (Mark 13:33-37)

"Someone else said, 'I will follow you sir; but first let me go and say good-bye to my family.' Jesus said to that person, 'Anyone who starts to plough and then keeps looking back is of no use to the Kingdom of God.'" (Luke 9:61-62)

Reflection

1. What helps you to maintain stability in your life and to be faithful to your commitments?
2. Do you know any individuals like Jimmy who made a radical change in their life? How did they do it?

Action

1. Volunteer to work with youth in distress.
2. Find a mentor who can counsel you whenever you feel overwhelmed by your commitments or when you are making an important decision in your life.

SAVANNA BABOON

Generosity

Baboons are among the most intelligent and sociable of all primates. They are also the most helpful and generous. Non-territorial, they live together in large troops ranging from eight to two hundred members. Females band together for life with their sisters and their offspring while males move in and out, protecting them and helping take care of the young, whether they are the actual father or not.

While there is a definite hierarchy within both male and female troops, they will come to one another's rescue when sick or in danger. Even lions are unable to penetrate this cooperative defense shield. Although there is competition for food and dominance, jealousy among baboons is rare. Females will allow both dominant and subordinate males to mate with them, and males will assist any member of a troop in distress. Each female has several favorite males with whom she roosts, socializes, and mates although she doesn't ignore others. These favorites play a godfather role with the young, which involves holding, carrying, grooming, and food-sharing. Godfathers also protect the young and assist subordinate females and their young to get their share of food, care, and attention. Such helpfulness and generosity have enabled baboons to become the most geographically widespread of African primates.

Ostriches, Dung Beetles, and Other Spiritual Masters

I found this same trait among my neighbors in Zimbabwe and Mozambique. During the struggle for independence in Rhodesia (present-day Zimbabwe), many fled to neighboring Mozambique. Food was scarce in the refugee camps deep in the forests of Mozambique, yet some of the women saved special treats for me, such as a piece of sugarcane or a candy bar. They told me later that they feared I would get sick on the meager diet of the camps and did what they could to keep me healthy, including boiling water for me to drink.

When I lived with another religious sister in Tafara township, our neighbors formed a protective shield around us, guarding us against theft or harassment. When our car was stolen not long after we moved in, the neighborhood youth tracked down the thief and returned the car to us. This recovery became a legend in the township, where stolen property was seldom seen again!

Jesus praises generosity and helpfulness throughout the Gospels. He speaks of the widow's mite and the lost coin. He chides the rich man who fails to help the beggar at his gate and lauds the Samaritan who stopped to help the man who was beaten, robbed, and left by the side of the road.

Jesus' own life offers numerous examples of responding generously to the needs of others. He feeds the crowd that comes to listen to him, saying: "I am filled with compassion for these people; they have already followed me for three days and now have nothing to eat. I do not want to send them away fasting, or they may faint on the way" (Matthew 15:32).

Jesus heals the sick and troubled who appeal to him for assistance and exhorts his followers to do the same. His story about the good shepherd tells of a kind and generous response to the most weak and needy among us: "The good shepherd gives his life for the sheep" (John 10:11).

The need for generosity goes beyond helping our neighbor at home. In our globalized world, the gap between rich and poor continues to grow. The response to global disasters, such as the tsunami in Southeast Asia and the droughts that continue to plague the African continent, is most encouraging. Well-known personalities who have access to wealth and prominence such as Oprah Winfrey, Stephen Lewis, Jimmy Carter, and Bill and Melinda Gates are using their resources to fight poverty and disease, provide education, and promote the rights of women and children in Africa. Each single action makes a difference.

Religious communities and nonprofit organizations are fortunate to have generous donors and sponsors who make our work possible. With the support of friends and relatives, I established a scholarship fund for girls in Zimbabwe that has enabled many young women to get an education. One of the recipients was Martha, a young woman who fled an abusive uncle who wanted to take her as a second wife. Her scholarship allowed her to attend a sewing course and provided her with a sewing machine on graduation. She now is married and has a son whom she helps to support with the clothes she makes.

My father used to tell me that whatever you give away, you get back in abundance. He was right! Generosity seldom goes unrewarded. It is also the hallmark of our Christian faith. As Jesus reminds us, "Whatever you did to the least of my brothers and sisters, you did it to me" (Matthew 25:40).

Scripture

"Do not deny the poor his food and do not make the person who looks at you with pleading eyes wait. Do not sadden the hungry person nor annoy anyone who is in need. . . . Do not drive away the beggar who is weighed down with afflictions, nor turn away your face from the poor; do not snub the needy or give anyone a reason to curse you." (Sirach 4:1-5)

"But a Samaritan, too, was going that way, and when he came upon the man, he was moved with compassion. He went over to him and treated his wounds with oil and wine and wrapped them with bandages. Then he put him on his own mount and brought him to an inn where he took care of him." (Luke 10:25-37)

"Jesus looked up and saw rich people putting their gifts into the treasure box; he also saw a poor widow dropping in two small coins. And he said, 'Truly, I tell you, this poor widow put in more than all of them. For all gave an offering from their plenty, but she, out of her poverty, gave all she had to live on.'" (Luke 21:1-4)

Reflection

1. Have you ever been the recipient of the generosity of others? How did it help you? How did you show your gratitude?
2. How do you give to others? Through what channels? For what causes?

Action

1. Learn more about a cause that interests you and see how you can help, whether with time, money or personal involvement.

2. Look at the Web site of your faith tradition and learn about programs that will allow you to participate in assisting others both at home and abroad. Maryknoll's Web site (www.maryknoll.org) provides information about programs of the Maryknoll Sisters, the Maryknoll Fathers and Brothers, Maryknoll's Lay Missioners, and Maryknoll Affiliates.

SPOTTED HYENA

Laughter

A night in the African bush is a symphony of sounds under a canopy of dazzling stars. Nightjars warble a serenade while owls hoot in harmony. If you are lucky, you might hear the mighty roar of the lion claiming its prey, or the trumpeting of a bull elephant as it charges to a watering hole. More often than not, you will hear the cackling laughter of the hyena as it searches for its evening meal.

Dog-like carnivores, hyenas are related to civets and mongooses. Their bodies have evolved in ways that enable them to survive on the harsh African plain. Their shoulders and front legs are higher than their hindquarters, allowing them to crawl and squeeze into narrow tunnels. When running, their hind feet are thrown out sideways, conserving energy and allowing them to lope tirelessly at six miles per hour. Their teeth and jaws are strong enough to chew through bone, hoof, hides, and teeth, making them the garbage disposals of the savanna.

While hyenas have a bad reputation as scavengers, most breeds hunt their prey as well as clean up the remains that other carnivores leave behind. Without their very thorough cleansing process, disease and pollution could easily spread.

The "laughing hyena" is signaling excitement, perhaps inviting others to come and join the feast or warning them of danger. The spotted hyena is the most vocal of the carnivores,

with eleven different calls, including groans, whoops, grunts, growls, and giggles.

"Laughter is the best medicine," my mother used to tell me. Doctors have recently discovered the truth of this maxim, suggesting that a good laugh every day promotes mental and physical health. Perhaps that's why comedy is such a universal language.

I recall watching a Charlie Chaplin film at a rural training center on the shores of Lake Victoria, Tanzania. The largely illiterate audience of small-scale farmers and fishers were doubled over with laughter throughout the film. Chaplin's pantomime spoke to them as eloquently as to the northern audience for which it was produced.

Laughter is very common on

the African continent, even in times of hardship and trouble. In the refugee camps in Mozambique, for example, weekly cultural festivals were held in which youth showed off their talent. During the war for independence, poetry, drama, song, and dance entertained the camp for a day, helping us to forget our hunger and the dangers present in the surrounding forest, not only from wild animals but from enemy bombardment as well.

"Raising morale" was how these festivals were explained to me. Such morale boosting helped thousands of refugee children and their teachers to laugh and relax for a few hours, strengthening them for the week ahead. Nothing was more hilarious than watching me try to dance with them.

The Gospels also speak of such light-hearted intervals in the lives of Jesus and the apostles—wedding feasts, meals with friends, playing with children, and roasting fish on the beach. His enemies even chastised Jesus for not taking life more seriously. He advised them to celebrate while "the bridegroom" was in their midst. Worship services in Africa are genuine celebrations, complete with song, dance, and hearty laughter. The Christian community seems to sense the value of rejoicing at least one day a week to express the undying faith of the people in the constant presence of God in their midst, through all their trials and tribulations.

Scripture

"For John came fasting and people said: 'He is possessed.' Then the Son of Man came, he ate and drank, and people said: 'Look at this man! A glutton and drunkard, a friend of tax collectors and sinners!' Yet they will see that Wisdom did everything well." (Matthew 11:18-19)

"Come to me, all you who work hard and who carry heavy burdens and I will refresh you." (Matthew 11:28)

"Rejoice in the Lord, you who are just,
praise is fitting for the upright.
Give thanks to God on the harp and lyre,
Making melody and chanting praises.

Amid loud shouts of joy,
Sing to God a new song
And play the ten-stringed harp." (Psalm 33:1-3)

Reflection

1. What gives you joy? How do you express it?
2. How do you have fun?
3. Can you laugh at yourself?

Action

1. Organize a celebration at your home or church to acknowledge a blessing, such as the birth of a child, a promotion at work, a graduation from school, and so on.

2. Find something to make you laugh at least once a day.
3. Bring joy to others through visits, gifts, cartoons, clowning, or another source of fun and laughter.

THORN TREE (ACACIA)

Serenity

Nothing distinguishes the African plain as much as the graceful thorn tree, whose umbrella-shaped canopy stretches as far as the eye can see, offering protection from the scorching midday sun to countless animals, large and small. Zebra and wildebeest huddle next to impala, kudu, and eland; herds of elephants stand still as statues, flapping only their ears to chase away flies, while giraffes nibble at the leafy shelter overhead. Playtime and naptime often overlap, with the big cats resting in the shadows while their cubs tumble in the grass nearby. Life stands still, serene and majestic, catching its breath before the struggle for survival begins again.

The thorn tree, or acacia, grows abundantly on the grassy savanna south of the equator and covers about 40 percent of the African landscape. Needing little water, it can survive a long dry season, providing both sustenance and shade to a variety of species.

For Africa's wildlife, while the search for food and water is never ending, the afternoon nap represents the rhythm of the natural world. Nature seems to recognize the need to stop and recuperate before continuing the relentless struggle of life and death in this harsh environment, where only the strong, resilient, and adaptable survive.

The countless tribes of people who share this huge continent, three times the size of the United States, also respect the rhythms of nature. They too engage in an unending struggle to survive. Although Africa is rich in natural resources, the wealth seldom benefits the local populations whose leaders, in league with foreign companies, pocket the proceeds of the oil, gold, diamonds, emeralds, cobalt, chrome, copper, and countless other minerals and gems that make this a virtual Garden of Eden.

After toiling long hours in the heat, workers nap in the noonday sun. Reclining under trees or in the shade of walls and buildings, they ignore the traffic and passersby as they grab a few blissful moments of rest before returning to their work. In rural fields, farm laborers also pause for lunch, lying in the shade of a tree or a tractor. Women pause in their endless round of fetching wood and water to recline against the wall of their home for a few precious hours before the cycle of manual labor resumes. And each day, Christian and non-Christian alike take time to thank the Creator for the gifts of life, family, food, and friends.

In the midst of our hectic modern life, many yearn for the serenity of the Dalai Lama or a Thomas Merton. We long to take time out from the daily list of things to be done to replenish ourselves and to silence the inner chatter that makes us anxious and frazzled. Can we learn from the rhythm of nature to stop and be still when we are feeling overwhelmed? Can we eat outside under the trees rather than in a crowded, noisy cafeteria? Can we go for a walk or sit alone, resting our eyes and our brains? Can we listen to the birds and watch the squirrels at play rather than reading a book or a newspaper? Can we take time out, morning and evening, to say thanks to the Creator for the gifts of each day? Can we just take time, instead of rushing and running through our lives?

A missioner's life is very active. Yet Mother Mary Joseph, our foundress, insisted that we be contemplatives in action. While Maryknoll Sisters have a contemplative branch that is devoted solely to prayer, each of us is meant to take time out in our busy lives for meditation and prayer. "We have undertaken a most active, strenuous, wearing form of religious life, that of an apostle, and we find that no day is ever long enough for all the things we would crowd into it," she said, and went on to counsel us, "This life must at the same time be deeply, intensely spiritual. We are to be contemplatives in action if we are to be successful in our apostolate" (Mother Mary Joseph, 1944).

Jesus also led an active life, healing, preaching, and teaching about God's kingdom. Yet he also took time to rest and to pray. He understood the natural rhythm of life and used images from nature to explain his mission—the world of flowers, birds, wheat, seeds, sheep, pearls, fish, sunshine, and rain. The wind and the sea obeyed him. Children played at his feet. He relaxed with friends over a meal and visited with rich and poor alike. Artists of all nations and all times depict him in various poses, clothing, and cultural settings but almost all capture an inner fire and an outer serenity that still attract followers around the world. May we too experience the fruit of contemplation in action.

Scripture

"If anyone is thirsty, let her come to me; and let him who believes in me drink, for the Scripture says: Out of him shall flow rivers of living water." (John 7:37-38)

"I am the vine and you are the branches. As long as you remain in me and I in you, you bear much fruit; but apart from me you can do nothing. Whoever does not remain in me is like a branch that is thrown away and withers; and the withered branches are gathered and thrown into the fire and burned." (John 15:5-6)

"The Lord is my shepherd, I shall not want.
He makes me lie down in green pastures.
He leads me beside the still waters,
he restores my soul." (Psalm 23:1-3)

Reflection

1. How do you recuperate after a busy day?
2. What do you do when you feel overwhelmed by the pressures of life?
3. If you have pets, notice the rhythm of their days; how much time is spent playing, eating, and sleeping. What can you learn from them?

Action

1. Try beginning and ending each day with at least ten minutes of silent meditation and prayer.
2. Read books by the spiritual masters and discuss what you have learned from them with your family or with a friend. You can find good reading in your local bookstore, the library in your parish or community, or online. The series

from Orbis Books entitled the Modern Spiritual Masters includes titles by Henri Nouwen, Mother Teresa, Thomas Merton, and many others (see www .orbisbooks.com).

3. Keep a journal in which you write your thoughts and feelings each day.

VERVET MONKEY

Friendship

Vervets are the most common small monkeys of the African savanna. From Ethiopia to the Cape, these bundles of energy tumble, jump, climb, and run together in family groups of up to fifty members. Ever curious and playful, they can easily be seen sitting on the shoulder of a road or swinging from branch to branch in wooded areas. There is hardly a more endearing sight than a mother vervet with her baby clutched to her chest or riding on her back. It's not only the mother that looks after the young, however, since all members of the family compete to groom, cuddle, carry, and play with the new arrivals.

Within a few weeks of birth, babies expand their network of playmates and baby sitters, associating with older siblings as well as juveniles from other groups. They are weaned from their mothers by the time they are four months old and are foraging on their own by six months. Surrounded by age-mates and friends, the vervet is very sociable and communicates through a variety of gestures and sounds. Researchers have identified at least sixty distinct physical gestures and thirty-six vocal calls that vervets use to send messages to each other. Rarely, if ever, are they alone. A strong social network helps them to survive and to thrive.

I was reminded of the benefits of a strong social network when food and fuel were in short supply during the economic and political crisis in Zimbabwe. Without friends to let one know where to find the scarce commodities one could easily go without. In our need, we all started to think of one another and help one another. Bread, milk, and eggs became rare treats that were to be shared. Backyard gardens began to feed a network of friends and co-workers. Friends also helped encourage one another to laugh at some of the craziness of the situation rather than to sink into hopelessness and despair.

"We can take a lot of physical and even mental pain when we know that it truly makes us a part of the life we live together in the world," wrote Henri Nouwen. "But when we feel cut off from the human family, we quickly lose heart."* I think this is true. Yet we often overlook our friends or take them for granted. We sometimes behave as if we don't need or want any help but can manage fine on our own, thank you very much! We can even feel that we are weak and incapable if we rely too much on others. Individual-

---

* From Nouwen's *Making All Things New*, as quoted by Robert J. Wicks in *Touching the Holy* (Notre Dame, Ind.: Ave Maria Press, 1992), 93.

ism can be elevated to an ideal, and we can feel proud that we don't need anyone else in our lives.

This is a far cry from African society, which is built around the extended family. Aunts and uncles are called mother and father and often act as surrogate parents; cousins are known as brothers and sisters and are just as close. One seldom walks alone through life but rather is surrounded by a loving and caring network of close relatives and friends.

I grew up in such a family, with dozens of cousins and close ties between us all. Even though I live thousands of miles away, I try to stay connected to my relatives and to my friends from my childhood and teenage years. This wider network is like a safety net that helps me through the hard times and makes the good times even better.

Jesus also had close friends. Not only did he choose twelve people to share his ministry but he also had a wider circle of friends and followers. "Jesus loved Martha and her sister and Lazarus," John tells us (John 11:5). The story of Martha and Mary is a familiar one that is often used to show the conflict between the two sisters, one busy preparing the meal while the other sits conversing with Jesus, apparently not doing her share of the domestic work. If we focus instead on the fact that Jesus took time off from his ministry to relax with friends and enjoy a meal, we might learn to do the same.

Shortly before his passion and death, Jesus journeyed to Bethany to have a final meal with these close friends. In a foretaste of the Last Supper, Mary used the occasion to anoint the feet of Jesus with perfume and to wipe them with her hair. This loving and extravagant gesture was condemned by Judas Iscariot, who would betray Jesus only a few days later. "This perfume could have been sold and the money given to the poor," he declared in judgment. But Jesus reprimanded him.

I witnessed such a loving, extravagant gesture when a friend in Holland was dying of cancer. She had worked in Zimbabwe for many years before being elected to the leadership team of her religious community. When she learned that her cancer had spread and further treatment was not possible, she chose to come to Zimbabwe to see her friends for the last time. We said good-bye, surrounded by the beauty of the country that had been her home. Although she was often in great pain, she brought laughter and joy to us all. She gave away each and every piece of clothing she brought with her but most of all she gave us the gift of her presence for the last time.

Like the vervet monkey, who has many different ways to communicate, we too can learn to show our appreciation to those who matter in our lives.

Scripture

"Six days before the Passover, Jesus came to Bethany where he had raised Lazarus, the dead man, to life. Now they gave a dinner for him, and while Martha waited on them, Lazarus sat at the table with Jesus. Then Mary took a pound of costly perfume made from genuine nard and anointed the feet of Jesus, wiping them with her hair. And the whole house was filled with the fragrance of the perfume." (John 12:1-4)

"Near the cross of Jesus stood his mother, his mother's sister Mary, who was the wife of Cleophas, and Mary Magdala. When Jesus saw his mother and the disciple, he said to his mother, 'Woman, this is your son.' Then he said to the disciple, 'There is your mother.' And from that moment the disciple took her to his own home." (John 19:25-27)

Reflection

1. Who are your close friends? How do you keep in touch with them?
2. Have you ever experienced an extravagant gesture of love? Did you ever give another such a gesture?

Action

1. Get in touch with an old friend who has been missing from your life.
2. Let a friend know how much he or she means to you by doing something special with and for that person.

WARTHOG

Resourcefulness

A Kenyan folktale recounts that the warthog was created with long ivory tusks and the elephant was given very small curved ones. The elephant envied the warthog and tricked him into exchanging tusks. After they had traded, the warthog laughed and said that the elephant would always live in fear and danger, as it would be hunted for its beautiful tusks while the ugly warthog could live in peace.

This story reminds the listeners to be content with what we have received from God. It is a lesson against envy and jealousy. Certainly the warthog, a pig with tusks, is not very attractive or eye-catching, but it is a survivor. Warthogs are found throughout the African savanna and are able to survive by eating grass as well as roots and tubers. Its snout is like a shovel that can dig into the earth to find tasty bulbs and nutritious rhizomes. Its jaw is hinged, enabling the warthog to grind grass and fruits.

The female warthog becomes fertile at eighteen to nineteen months and gives birth to two to five offspring at a time after a gestation period of about five and a half months. The young remain in the burrow for the first six weeks, after which they accompany their mother everywhere, filing behind her in a fixed order. A parade of warthogs, walking single file, is a common and humorous sight throughout the continent.

Ostriches, Dung Beetles, and Other Spiritual Masters

Warthogs have learned how to survive even though they have some predators, including human beings, who find their meat very delicious. The warthog lives in burrows where it is safe from predators and also from the hot sun. The male uses its small tusks to protect its young and also to compete with other males for a mate. They do not impress by their looks or by their deeds, but they have learned to use the scarce resources around them to live. They do not even dig their own burrows, but use holes that have been excavated and abandoned by aardvarks.

I experienced such resourcefulness in camps of Zimbabwean refugees, hidden deep in the forests of neighboring Mozambique. Such camps housed thousands of men, women, and children who had fled the violence at home, bringing with them only the possessions they could carry on their heads—a few clothes, a blanket, a pot, and enough food for the journey. Arriving at their destination, they discovered that they had to fend for themselves. They planted gardens, dug pit latrines, and constructed houses from local bamboo and grass. Classes were held under the trees with students making desks and benches from bamboo poles. They used sticks as pencils and wrote their lessons in the dusty soil. Nothing was wasted. Empty tin cans were filled with paraffin and used as lamps, burlap sacks that had held grain were used to insulate the walls of the houses, and ashes from the cooking fires were used to clean the pit latrines.

This experience reinforced the training I had received from my parents. I grew up at the end of World War II when families were encouraged to save newspapers, old cans and bottles, and the remains of soap and fat from cooking. Monthly, my mother and I would deliver our savings to the local store, where they were recycled. This was long before there was an environmental movement that promoted recycling.

Living on a continent that has so much poverty and so many shortages, one also learns that everything is valuable and can be reused. Old bottles can be given to local clinics to hold medicine; newspapers are used for toilet paper; scraps of cloth and old clothing can be made into quilts and pillows; ends of candles can be melted down and combined to make new candles.

But it shouldn't take a war or shortages to encourage resourcefulness. The consumer societies of the industrialized North are not sustainable. The world's natural resources are finite and must be replenished or they will be exhausted. The United States and Europe, with 20 percent of the world's population, consume 80 percent of the world's resources. China and India are fast becoming consumer societies as well. Unless we learn to reduce consumption, the planet will die. Can we learn from the warthog to make the best use of the little that we have? Instead of envying those who have more, let us remember that the elephant, with its precious tusks, is becoming an endangered species while the warthog is safely roaming the African savanna.

Scripture

"Get yourselves purses that do not wear out, and make safe investments with God, where no thief comes and no moth destroys. For where your investments are, there will your heart be also." (Luke 12:33-34)

"Much will be required of the one who has been given much, and more will be asked of the one entrusted with more." (Luke 12:48)

"No servant can serve two masters. Either he does not like the one and is fond of the other, or he regards one highly and the other with contempt. You cannot give yourself both to God and to Money." (Luke 16:13)

Reflection

1. Have you ever had to improvise with what you had to create something new? How did it make you feel?
2. Have you ever gone without something you wanted, either because you couldn't afford it or because you were trying to live simply? How did it make you feel?
3. Do you recycle newspapers, bottles, cans, and other reusable products? Why or why not?

Action

1. Join an environmental group that encourages recycling and a simple lifestyle.
2. Analyze the advertisements in a magazine or newspaper that you receive. What is the message that is being propagated? How does it influence you? Is there something you can do to counteract the media's message that more is better?
3. Give up a meal each week and give the money you save to a local charity that feeds the hungry.

WEAVER BIRD

Creative Conflict Management

Weaver birds build their nests at the ends of very slim branches. These beautifully constructed homes sway and dangle with every breeze, and it often seems as if the branches are too weak to hold their weight. The entrance to the nest is at the bottom so the birds must fly up from below. As one watches the parent bird fluttering near the entrance with a treat for its babies, one wonders how the baby birds stay inside without falling to the ground.

This feat of architectural daring and originality has a very practical purpose. It is intended to prevent snakes and monkeys from entering the nests and eating the eggs. These predators are not able to maintain their grip on the thin branches and fall to the ground if they attempt to reach the tempting nests. The weaver bird does not attack its enemies but outwits them.

In our peace-building program at Silveira House, the leadership training center where I worked in Harare, we teach that the common responses to conflict or differences are fight, flight, and flow. Fight is an aggressive position in which we strike back when hurt, while flight is a tendency to avoid conflict by escaping or ignoring it, like the ostrich who lowers its head to avoid detection. We encourage participants to adopt a flow approach, which means accepting conflict as part of everyday life and choosing to

learn from it rather than adopting an aggressive response or withdrawing. We encourage them to be as creative as the weaver bird in preventing conflict and avoiding unnecessary danger.

I also served as a member of the board of a human rights organization in Zimbabwe that counsels and provides medical treatment to the victims of violence. Our training was put to the test on many occasions as the organization was frequently attacked in the state-owned media, and its board and staff threatened with arrest. We debated how best to respond to this habitual harassment and eventually chose to dialogue with the officials concerned rather than issuing a rebuttal through the media, taking legal action or letting ourselves be intimidated into closing down the organization for fear of imprisonment, banning, or worse.

We overcame our fear and approached those who were attacking us. When we eventually met face to face, we were able to break through the exaggerated propaganda and put a name and a face on what we were trying to do. The government officials were also able to ask questions and voice their concerns. Although the officials still were not happy with the work we were doing, the government ceased the frontal attacks and the staff was able to continue to assist the victims of violence in relative peace and security. Although the government continued to seek other ways to close down the organization, we no longer lived in fear of the unknown. Perhaps both sides had been able to remove the label of "enemy" of the unknown other. We were now able to voice our differences openly and to seek clarification when misunderstandings arose.

I recall the story of Jesus outwitting the Roman rulers who sent someone to trap him into claiming to be a rival to Caesar. Jesus did not refuse to answer the question nor did he attack his opponents. Rather he outwitted them by acknowledging the authority of Caesar while putting limits on his power. "Give to Caesar the things that are Caesar's and to God the things that are God's." Anyone who is forced to give false allegiance to human power can learn from Jesus' example. When facing Pontius Pilate, Jesus again clarified that God is the source and the limit of all earthly power: "You would have no power over me unless it had been given you from above; therefore the one who handed me over to you is even more guilty" (John 19:11).

If earthly rulers ask their subjects to break God's law, the people are obliged to refuse. Thomas More lost his life rather than accept the king's flouting of the law of God. War resisters, whistle blowers, and those who question unjust laws are all witnesses to creative conflict resolution. We may not always win. Successful living, however, is not about winning or losing but about maintaining or restoring relationships in the wake of disagreements.

Scripture

"If your sister or brother has sinned against you, go and point out the fault in private, and if s/he listens to you, then you have won over your sister/brother." (Matthew 18:15)

"They sent to Jesus some Pharisees with members of Herod's party, with the purpose of trapping him in his own words. They came and said to Jesus, 'Tell us, is it against the Law to pay taxes to Caesar? Should we pay them or not?' But Jesus saw through their trick and answered, 'Why are you testing me: Bring me a silver coin and let me see it.' They brought him one and Jesus asked, 'Whose head is this, and whose name?' They answered, 'Caesar's.' Then Jesus said, 'Give back to Caesar what belongs to Caesar, and to God what belongs to God.' And they were greatly astonished." (Mark 12:13-17)

Reflection

1. Give examples of those who choose dialogue in the face of opposing views.
2. Can you recall times when you used the "flow" approach when you differed with others rather than attacking or fleeing? What happened?
3. In extreme provocation such as a terrorist attack, rape, or murder, is it realistic to seek for dialogue and understanding with the "enemy"? How would one go about it?
4. What are some alternatives to "going to war" when a nation feels threatened by another nation or group of people, such as the "war against terror"?

Action

1. The next time that you disagree with another or face a situation of conflict, seek to initiate dialogue to find out what interests or needs that you might have in common with the other person.
2. Join an advocacy group that shares your concerns about a specific issue in order to bring change through peaceful means.

WILDEBEEST

Cooperation

The wildebeest is the most sociable of mammals with hoofs, called ungulates in scientific terms. A large, bearded antelope with short grey or brownish hair, the wildebeest is neither graceful nor beautiful. With a hump on its back and short, cowlike horns, it is large and slow, becoming prey to lion and hyena alike. What it lacks in looks, it makes up for in sociability and group protection strategies.

The wildebeest is best known for its annual migration across Tanzania's Serengeti Plains when almost one million beasts move to greener pastures. The dangerous journey sees thousands plunging over steep precipices, swimming through flooded rivers, and dodging crocodiles and other predators waiting to take advantage of this huge moving feast. The migration coincides with the mating season when approximately 250,000 bulls compete for 750,000 cows during a three-week period.

The wildebeest is constantly on the move, in search of the grass on which it feeds about one-third of each day. It grazes on the wide-open plains where there is no place to hide. In order for the young to survive, the wildebeest has evolved a unique solution. Almost the whole herd gives birth to its young at the same time, at the start of the rains when food is plentiful. The newborn calves stay close to their mothers and are protected by the *entire herd moving together. The most important advantage of a short birthing season is to produce a glut for predators and also to assure cover for newborns within the maternity bands. While many newborns are taken, at least half are able to survive through this mutual aid scheme.*

Such cooperation is rare in both animal and human endeavors. When it happens, it is magic. In 2006, the Maryknoll Sisters congregation organized a year-long commemoration of the fiftieth anniversary of the death of our foundress, Mary Josephine (Mollie) Rogers. We chose several unique activities to recall her contribution to the worldwide church and to the universal call to mission. Each event planned for the year required endless preparation and the cooperation of every member of our community and every department at our center in Ossining, New York.

As co-chair of a global forum that brought together speakers from around the world to address issues such as peace and reconciliation, ethics, human and environmental rights, and economic justice, I understood the need to cooperate firsthand. The logistics of organizing transport, communication, food, and accommodations were daunting, but each and every aspect seemed to fall into place as Maryknoll Sisters around the world helped contact speakers and obtain visas and tickets, while others provided hospitality and made guests feel at home when they arrived in New York.

Not a single person declined the invitation to assist in one form or another. Some scrubbed and cleaned until our center was sparkling. Others cooked and baked to provide a sumptuous lunch for more than three hundred visitors, and some wrote press releases and hosted the media while others welcomed visitors and led them to their

Wildebeest—Cooperation

139

respective workshops. It was a miracle of coordination and cooperation. The three co-chairs could only marvel that such a complex event unfolded so gracefully. One could truly feel the spirit of Mother Mary Joseph drawing us together and enabling us to sacrifice individually for the good of the whole. This spirit infused the entire year, offering a glimpse of the power of a common vision and a unified response.

Such unity and cooperation are almost the opposite of the world as we know it, where war, poverty, and inequality create enemies and where competition replaces cooperation. In this world, there are winners and losers, victors and vanquished. Yet Jesus left us a vision of God's reign where the lion and lamb lie down together and where rich and poor share the heavenly banquet together.

Some might see this image as utopian and unrealistic, but the followers of Jesus take this message seriously and work to bring it to life in the here and now. Some devote their lives to nonviolent change; others work to save the planet, to heal the sick, and to protect the rights of the most vulnerable. There are many ways to work for the coming of the reign of God. If all those working for change could cooperate like the wildebeest perhaps we might succeed in making the world a better place!

Scripture

> "See, the body is one, even if formed by many members, but not all of them with the same function. The same with us: being many, we are one body in Christ, depending on one another. Let each one of us, therefore, serve according to our different gifts." (Romans 12:4-8)

"The whole community of believers were one in heart and mind. None considered as their own what belonged to them; but rather they shared all things in common." (Acts 4:32)

Reflection

1. Have you ever experienced an example of cooperation to achieve a common goal? When was it? What happened?
2. Have you ever experienced an instance when people pulled in different directions and failed to achieve their goal? When was it? What happened?
3. Do you know any people who seem to have a gift for bringing others together, for bridging differences and for promoting cooperation? Who are they? How do they manage to use this gift?

Action

1. Invite others to join you in a project to improve the neighborhood where you live, the place where you work, or the school that you attend. It can be something as simple as filling a pothole in the road, planting flowers in an open space, or clearing away papers and trash that have accumulated. The activity is less important than the interaction among the participants.
2. Join a group or a committee at your local church that works together for a common cause such as feeding the hungry, preparing the weekly church service, or visiting the sick.

ZEBRA

Originality

The stripes on a zebra are as unique and individual as a person's fingerprints. The width and shape of stripes vary in different subspecies of zebras as well as between zebras of the same species. No two are alike! Zebras generally mate for life. The filly begins ovulating between one and two years of age and will stay until death with the first stallion to impregnate her. Stallions are very protective of their mares and their offspring, defending them against predators such as the lion and hyena.

Each stallion gradually accumulates a harem in which a strict hierarchy is enforced with the first mate taking precedence over the second, the second over the third, and so on. This order is followed whenever the herd files from one pasture or water hole to another. When family members become separated, the family stallion goes looking and calling for them and the whole herd will adjust its pace to accommodate sick or crippled members. Zebras recognize each other and can identify members of the same family, from the oldest to the newly born, each with its unique markings.

N*o Two Alike* was the title of a popular book about the Maryknoll Sisters written several years ago by Sr. Maria del Rey, a prolific author who had been a journalist before she joined the congregation. The book told the stories of about twenty sisters, each with a unique background, upbringing, personality, and ministry. It stressed the richness of the diversity within the community and the importance of being oneself and using one's unique gifts in the service of others.

There seems to be a trend in modern society to imitate and to look like everyone else. Globalization is spreading the same trends worldwide. Young people in New York, Moscow, or Tokyo wear the same brands of jeans and shoes; they listen to the same music and watch the same films. This kind of mono-culture threatens to eradicate the originality of local languages, traditions, and cultures.

Human languages and cultures are dying out even faster than animal species. It is estimated that 426 languages are nearly extinct while 52 have only one native

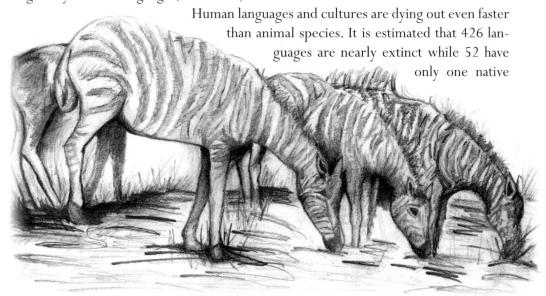

speaker remaining. Of the approximately six thousand languages in the world, 55 percent of the world's population speak just fifteen of them. Some linguists predict that 50 percent of the world's languages will have died out by the end of the twenty-first century if no action is taken to protect them.*

While linguistic changes and adaptation are a normal process, what is frightening is the artificial extinction of so many so quickly. Since culture is embedded in a language, this extinction threatens to erase cultural identity as well. This reality was brought home to me very forcefully when I met the Tonga people of Zimbabwe. Living along the shores of the Zambezi River, the Tonga subsisted on fishing and hunting until the mid-1950s, when they were moved to make way for a large dam that was built to harness the water of the Zambezi for hydroelectric power to serve Zimbabwe and Zambia. The Tonga community, which lived on both sides of the river, was split in two with the Zimbabwean Tonga being resettled far from the river on barren land that yields little food.

When I visited them to discover the needs of the people, I was surprised by what I learned. We thought that the people might mention the lack of food, jobs, and decent housing or perhaps their distance from the river. Instead, they unanimously lamented the failure to teach the Tonga language in the local schools. "Our ancestors are crying because our children can't speak their language," said one chief. Another elder said that he dreams and prays in Tonga but must use foreign languages in his daily life. Although they were poor and they were hungry, these were not the issues they raised. They put their identity as a people first.

---

* Statistics found in Isaac Mumpande, *Silent Voices* (Harare: Silveira House with Weaver Press, 2006).

When they lobbied to have their language taught in schools in areas where they are the dominant group, some members of government objected, claiming that this would create division in the country. The Tonga replied that denying them the right to be themselves was what was creating the tension and division between different ethnic groups. They convinced the officials that by promoting the uniqueness of each ethnic group, they would help to create harmony and unity. Division and discord are caused by discrimination and inequality, not by respect and tolerance, they successfully argued.

If we look closely at the armed conflicts taking place in the twenty-first century, we can see that many are caused by a sense of being left out and overlooked or of being dominated by a larger and more powerful group. Whether the differences are between Arabs and Jews, as in the Middle East, between Catholic and Protestants in Northern Ireland, or between Hutu and Tutsi in Rwanda, we can see the consequences of a feeling of rejection or lack of respect.

Politicians sometimes exploit cultural and linguistic differences to win votes. Once they are in power, they reward their followers by monopolizing state resources and wealth that should benefit all members of society. Such inequality and injustice are often at the root of ethnic conflict, as was recently experienced in Kenya.

Our multicultural world challenges us to accept diversity and to be open to differences. Many corporations and religious communities include diversity training in their orientation programs to build a sense of unity and teamwork among their members. Unless we understand and accept our differences, there is little hope of achieving peace and unity.

Can we recognize that, like the zebra, our uniqueness is a gift? Let us celebrate the variety of languages, cultures, customs, and backgrounds on our wonderfully diverse planet Earth!

Scripture

"Peter was still speaking when the Holy Spirit came upon all who listened to the Word. And the believers of Jewish origin who had come with Peter were amazed, 'Why! God gives and pours the Holy Spirit on foreigners also!' And indeed this happened: they heard them speaking in tongues and praising God." (Acts 10:44-46)

"Here are Parthians, Medes and Elamites and residents of Mesopotamia, Judea and Cappadocia, Pontus and Asia, Phrygia, Pamphylia, Egypt and the parts of Libya belonging to Cyrene, and visitors from Rome, both Jews and foreigners who accept Jewish beliefs, Cretans and Arabians: and all of us hear them proclaiming in our own language what God, the Savior, does." (Acts 2:9-11)

Reflection

1. Have you ever been in a place where no one spoke your native language? How did you feel?

2. Have you learned a second or third language? How do people respond when you speak to them in their native language?
3. Do you live in a multicultural neighborhood? What feels good about it? What makes you feel strange or out of place?

Action

1. Reflect on the sense of your own identity and write in your journal what it feels like to be you, how you came to understand your uniqueness, what is at the core of who you are, what you can live without, what is essential to you for maintaining your sense of self.
2. Share with someone you know from a different background or a different ethnic group and see what is similar and what is different in your respective self-understanding and self-awareness.

SOURCES

Bailey, Simon. *The Well Within: Parables for Living and Dying.* London: Darton, Longman & Todd, 1996.

Bould, Geoffrey, ed. *Conscience Be My Guide: An Anthology of Prison Writings.* London: Zed Books, 2005.

Christian Community Bible. 18th ed. Chicago: Claretian Publications, 1995.

Estes, Richard D. *The Safari Companion: A Guide to Watching African Mammals.* Harare: Tutorial Press, 1993.

Mandela, Nelson. *Long Walk to Freedom: The Autobiography of Nelson Mandela.* Boston: Little, Brown, 1994.

Mumpande, Isaac. *Silent Voices.* Harare: Silveira House with Weaver Press, 2006.

National Audubon Society. *Field Guide to African Wildlife.* New York: Alfred A. Knopf, 1995.

Nyerere, Julius K. *Freedom and Development.* London: Oxford University Press, 1973.

Schreiter, Robert J. *Reconciliation: Mission and Ministry in a Changing Social Order.* Maryknoll, N.Y.: Orbis Books, 1992.

Tutu, Desmond. *God Has a Dream: A Vision of Hope for Our Time.* New York: Doubleday/Image, 2005.

————. *No Future without Forgiveness.* New York: Doubleday/Image, 1999.

Vanier, Jean. *I Walk with Jesus.* New York: Paulist Press, 1986.

Wicks, Robert J. *Touching the Holy.* Notre Dame, Ind.: Ave Maria Press, 1992.